THE EPISTLE TO THE ROMANS

NEW TESTAMENT FOR SPIRITUAL READING

VOLUME 12

Edited by

John L. McKenzie, S.J.

THE EPISTLE
TO THE ROMANS

KARL KERTELGE

CROSSROAD · NEW YORK

2580

1981
The Crossroad Publishing Company
575 Lexington Avenue, New York, NY 10022

Originally published as *Der Brief an die Römer*
© 1970 by Patmos-Verlag
from the series *Geistliche Schriftlesung*
edited by Wolfgang Trilling
with Karl Hermann Schelke and Heinz Schürmann

English translation © 1972 by Sheed and Ward, Ltd.
Translated by Francis McDonagh

Library of Congress Catalog Card Number: 81-68170
ISBN: 0-8245-0121-7

PREFACE

The Epistle to the Romans is the most densely theological work of the New Testament. Even in the first generation of the Christian community questions had arisen for which the simple proclamation of the gospel had no answer. The Christ event became the object of reflection, and from the reflection the stance of the Christian life was more sharply defined. The Good News which had been first proclaimed and believed in Palestinian towns and villages demanded a more complex response in the great cities of the Hellenistic-Roman world. Paul, the learned rabbi who was the Apostle of the Gentiles, was the best equipped man of whom we know to interpret the gospel and the Christian life to the mixed or largely Gentile churches of the large cities. What he produced in this epistle was a theological event, and it has set off other events in subsequent history. The expositions of the Epistle to the Romans produced by Martin Luther in the sixteenth century and Karl Barth in the twentieth century initiated revolutionary theological developments the effects of which are still felt.

The modern reader of the epistle is sure to feel himself in a strange religious world. The controversy which lies at the base of the epistle plays no part in his own religious life. If he has heard of the near schism in the apostolic church between Jewish Christians and Gentile Christians, he is not likely to know what the issues were. He is vaguely acquainted with modern anti-Semitism and he can easily place Paul in the anti-Semitic camp; this is to misunderstand Paul seriously. The only difference Paul recognizes between Jews and Christians is a theological difference, and theology has never meant anything in anti-Semitism.

The issue which divided Jewish and Gentile Christians was the claim of Jewish Christians that Gentiles had to become Jews in order to be Christians; they maintained that all Christians

5

were bound to the observance of the whole Law of Moses, symbolized by the circumcision of males. Very probably this position was generally accepted without reflection in the primitive Church, and Paul was probably the first to question it. We do not know what basis Jewish Christians may have found in the memory of the words of Jesus; no sayings of this kind are preserved in the gospels. Paul, as far as we know, was the first to perceive the profound theological implications in the thesis of the Jewish Christians and he sets them forth in the Epistle to the Romans.

The fundamental question was whether God's total and exclusive saving act of all men had been accomplished in Jesus Christ. If Jews were more saved than Gentiles and if Gentiles had to reach that salvation which was possible through Judaism before they could be reached by God's saving act in Christ, then God's saving act in Christ lacked universal efficacy. To Paul as to us this was an intolerable idea, and one believes that it must have been intolerable to primitive Christians once it was stated. Yet not only Jewish but Gentile Christians were fascinated by the belief that the God who saved in Christ was revealed only to the Jews, that only the Jews had received in the Law the revealed will of God as to how they should live, and that the Christ himself was a Jew who preached only to Jews. To say that Judaism did not save seemed like saying that God did not save, or that God had rejected his own work.

Paul better than anyone else saw that Judaism of his time, the religion in which he had been reared, had become a sect, at home only within certain ethnic and cultural limitations. The Scriptures themselves manifested a destiny of Israelite revelation which went beyond sectarian boundaries; the one God of all men must ultimately speak to all men, but must men become Jews in order to hear him? Up to Paul's time Judaism had done nothing to realize its larger destiny except in Jesus Christ, who was the fulfillment of Judaism and the word of God addressed to all men.

Hence Paul sets himself to argue that all men are hopelessly sunk in sin from which only God through Christ delivers them. Every Jew would listen with approval to Paul's charge that the Gentile world is morally corrupt; they must have been shocked when he turned his argument against the Jews themselves to show that they too were in desperate need. This universal bond of sin Paul traces back to the very origins of the human race—not without some ingenious exegesis. By the same ingenuity he shows that God's saving act began not with Moses, who gave Israel the Law, but with Abraham, who attained God by faith. Faith is what Jesus demands, and what all men, Jews or Gentiles, must yield; and it is all they must yield.

But if the Jews, like the Gentiles, are hopelessly sunk in sin, what is to be said of the Law, the revealed will of God concerning how man should live? Paul meets this by affirming that the Law imposed obligations that man was unable to meet. It was therefore a revelation of sin rather than a revelation of the saving power of God. The Law is annulled by the gospel, which gives man the ability to fulfill the will of God. The annulment of the Law does not mean the annulment of the moral will of God. Paul refers—rather briefly, it seems—to a basic theme of the gospel. It is love which fulfills the entire Law; this is what Jesus has revealed. And this is also the basis of Paul's theme of Christian freedom. The Christian life is not measured by a set of obligations which can be counted and weighed. The duty of love is simple and at the same time it is never perfectly fulfilled. When the Christian sees that his one obligation is the obligation of love he can never say that he has done all that he is obliged to do. The freedom of the Christian from the numerous and complex obligations of the Law is freedom to do something to which the law of Judaism did not oblige him. He need not feel overwhelmed by the casuistry of the Law, but need only look at his neighbor and ask himself whether he has loved as much as he is able.

The hopelessness of the human condition in general is affirmed by Paul of the human person in particular. It is not only the human condition of social pressure which keeps man from fulfilling the will of God, it is pressure from within each individual man. To this pressure theology has given the name of concupiscence. This pressure also is overcome by the saving act of God in Christ; and here Paul introduces the theme of baptism, which is a new birth to a new life and new powers which man does not have as long as he is subject to Sin and Death. Paul here seems to borrow a theme from Judaism; the rabbis regarded the circumcision of the Gentile proselyte as a legal death which released the proselyte from all obligations, even debts and marriage. The emergence of a new person was shown by the presentation of a new name. Paul develops the theme of a new birth to a new life far beyond the point of rabbinical teaching. The Christian by baptism becomes a new man in Christ, enabled to exhibit the life of Jesus in his body.

Paul was aware that his position towards Jewish Christians would not be well received by them. Not all of his readers have understood that his position was painful to himself too. One must refer to the text and the commentary of chapters 9–11 to pursue this subject fully, and even then one realizes that Paul never reached a satisfactory solution of this problem. His people were the chosen people, a fact he could not and did not wish to deny. That as a group they did not recognize their Messiah was the last mystery in the career of a people whose history from the beginning had been mysterious. Paul affirmed his belief that God was faithful to his people, but how he would have ultimately shown his fidelity Paul did not pretend to know. Had the relations of Jews and Christians been governed on the Christian side by the theology of Paul, much of what is the shame of Christians would never have happened.

These few lines do not suggest that the Epistle to the Romans is easy, and it is not easy. The reader must approach the epistle not only with humility and openness, but also with some degree of knowledge. Kertelge's commentary will furnish him much of the knowledge which he needs. Read with humility and an informed mind, the Epistle is one of the most rewarding works of the New Testament. JOHN L. McKENZIE

OUTLINE

THE OPENING OF THE LETTER
(1:1-7)

The letter opens according to the pattern current in the ancient world: "The writer . . . to the recipient . . . greetings." In our letter, however, this pattern is totally disrupted by a series of clauses and complex ideas introduced between the name of the writer and the description of the recipients. It should be noted that these additional elements give further details about the writer; they are clearly meant to help Paul to introduce himself. These additions deserve particular attention, as they contain in very concentrated form Paul's theology of his vocation and the essential features of his gospel.

The Writer, Paul (1:1-7)

His Vocation (1:1)

1Paul, a servant of Jesus Christ, called to be an apostle, set apart for the gospel of God . . .

Paul introduces himself. He is "a servant of Jesus Christ," "called to be an apostle" and (a reference to his mission) "set apart for the gospel of God." These three details are not merely placed side by side, but connected; each helps to bring out the meaning of the others.

Paul describes himself as "a servant of Jesus Christ," not merely out of self-depreciation and certainly not out of servility—that would run counter to his sense of freedom—but because of the way he sees his role as an apostle: he is in the service of Jesus Christ. This is Old Testament language. In the psalms the worshipper speaks of himself as the servant of Yahweh to acknowledge his creaturely dependence, and the expression became in time a recognized title in the mouths of important Old Testament figures. It would be a mistake to think of the ancient slave system as the main influence on Paul's language here; more important is his deep attachment to the ideas of the Old Testament and Judaism. Paul also uses the term " servant " as a title in Gal. 1:10 and Phil. 1:1. It is in the same class as *diakonos* (variously translated in RSV as " servants," 1 Thess. 3:2; 1 Cor. 3:5; 2 Cor. 6:4; 11:15, and " minister," 2 Cor. 3:6; Col. 1:7, 23, 25; 4; 7) and *apostolos*, which is Paul's most common description of himself (cf. Rom. 11:13; Gal. 1:1; 1 Cor. 1:1; 9:1f.; 15:9; 2 Cor. 1:1).

Paul is an apostle because of a " call ": God " called me through his grace " (Gal. 1:15). Paul is always conscious that being an apostle means being bound by the call he has received from God, but there is no sign that he feels this tie as a limitation on his personal freedom or a loss of freedom. God's call means for him, first, the new possibility offered by Christ of achievement in a life of service, and consequently his own personal fulfillment. Paul devotes the new life he has received from Christ to the service of men. That is his calling.

His Gospel (1:2-4)

²(the gospel) *which he promised beforehand through his prophets in the holy scriptures,* ³*the gospel concerning his Son, who was descended from David according to the flesh* ⁴*and designated Son of God in power according to the Spirit of holiness by his resurrection from the dead, Jesus Christ our Lord.*

In a few short phrases Paul sets out the essence of the gospel he is called to preach. Verse 2 gives more detail about the relationship between the gospel and God. We learn that Paul's gospel is " the gospel of God " which was announced beforehand or, alternatively, that what was previously announced for the future is now proclaimed by Paul as a reality in the present. The reference to " his prophets in the holy scriptures " should not be taken too literally; we do not have to ask which prophets and which Old Testament texts are meant. The contrast here is not between the Old Testament and the new, but between God's previous preaching through the prophets and the Christ-event. Obviously both are revelation, but the point is that revelation is a single process. It is only through his experience of faith in the present, in the light of the Christ-event, that Paul can say that God has proclaimed all this in the past through his prophets in the scriptures. The " advance preaching " of the gospel refers not so much to particular Old Testament prophecies as to the beginning and source of the gospel, beyond all history, in God.

The content of the gospel is Jesus Christ. Verses 3 and 4 explain the position in the words of a primitive Christian creed. It is likely that there are primitive Christian traditions, going back beyond Paul in a number of passages in the Epistle, even where Paul does not explicitly acknowledge them, especially in 3:24-6; 4:24f.; 10:9f.

The typical parallel construction of a creed can be seen quite clearly in the two subordinate elements of the description in 1:3-4, " who was descended from . . . and designated." The two parts speak of Christ from two points of view. He was born as a son of David, he is now in power, designated Son of God, " by his resurrection from the dead." The last phrase does not imply a limitation of Christ's dignity as Son; the qualification " by his resurrection " refers rather to the full exercise of that dignity. There is a point in the juxtaposition of the two statements. Jesus is son of David and he is Son of God; the second transcends the first, as the additional contrast between " flesh " and " spirit " makes clear. These two words describe the visible and earthly and the heavenly and eschatological existence of Jesus. It is noteworthy that Paul adds something of his own to the title of Christ in the traditional formula: " Jesus Christ our Lord." He also adds " his Son " at the beginning as an introduction. The accumulation of titles should not, however, give us the impression that Paul's main interest is in a detailed and comprehensive description of the status of Jesus rather than in the Christ-event. The essential content of any preaching of Christ is the affirmation that the Jesus of our creed is the Christ in whom the world achieves its salvation and who already exercises his rule in his believing community.

His Work Among the Gentiles (1:5–6)

5(Jesus Christ) through whom we have received grace and apostleship to bring about the obedience of faith for the sake of his name among all the nations, 6including yourselves who are called to belong to Jesus Christ. . . .

The subject, as in verse 1, is the role of an apostle. Paul understands his apostolic office as " grace." This is the grace given to him specifically for his apostolic mission, but in its essence it is the very grace of justification and being a Christian which is given to every believer, the new life-giving relationship of the believer to Jesus Christ. It is simply its action in Paul that is different, related to his mission in the service of the gospel. The " grace of apostleship " bears fruit in the " obedience of faith " to which it leads " among all the nations." The goal of the gospel preaching is that " obedience " which consists in faith in Jesus and in which Jesus' demands are met by loving surrender.

Paul is in a special way the missionary to " the nations." We need to understand this term in the wide sense which includes the Jews living among the Gentiles—this is very important for Paul's missionary methods. The most important words in the passage, however, are " among all." Paul wants to stress the universal applicability of his gospel and the consequent scope of his apostleship. Through the obedience of faith which Paul brings about among the Gentiles, the " name " of Jesus is honored. This means more than an external recognition or worship of Jesus (" his name " here means his " person "), and stands in fact for the central purpose of the preaching. The gospel preaching only takes effect when men obey Jesus, when they accept his death as a saving event and acknowledge his claim in the present to be the risen and exalted Lord. Paul's task as an apostle is to bring this about.

Paul is sent in a special way to preach the gospel among the Gentiles, and therefore has a special message also for those in Rome. They are a part of the nations who are called to the obedience of faith. As he has described himself as "called to be an apostle," so he now addresses the Roman Christians as those "who are called to belong to Jesus Christ."

The Recipients: the Romans (1:7a)

7aTo all God's beloved in Rome, who are called to be saints. . .

The recipients of the letter have already been mentioned in verse 6 but, in accordance with the conventions, it is only now that they are addressed by name. Paul addresses them as "God's beloved" and "[those] called to be saints," descriptions which he often applies to Christians especially at the beginning of letters. These phrases are much more than a pious flourish. "God's beloved" are Christians as such, who have come near to God through Jesus Christ. The expression "called to be saints" also has theological significance: Christians owe their existence as Christians to the call they have received. "Called" in verses 1–7 becomes a theme—the word appears three times—associating the apostle and his readers from the start.

Greeting (1:7b)

7bGrace to you and peace from God our Father and the Lord Jesus Christ.

Paul adopts the usual Jewish form of greeting in a letter (cf. Jude 1:2) but modifies it characteristically. The first word of the greeting stresses the "grace-event" in which God approaches men. Through the fundamental revelation of grace in the death and resurrection of Jesus, peace is given, as a gift "from God our Father and the Lord Jesus Christ."

THE BODY OF THE LETTER
(1:8—5:32)

Introduction (1:8–17)

The formal greeting over, Paul now addresses himself directly
and in a most complimentary fashion to his readers. He still has
to establish a connection with them, and does this now in the
conventional compliment he pays to the Christian community
in Rome: your faith is known throughout the world. This is his
reason for giving thanks to God. After the thanksgiving comes
the request to God. Paul has prayed so often in the past that he
might be enabled to visit Rome. Verses 11–15 describe from
various points of view the intention which he is about to carry
out. In verse 14 he says that his real reason is his missionary
obligation—this is his fundamental motive and all other reasons
follow from it. The passage as a whole leaves the impression
that Paul is trying to establish a connection because there has so
far been none.

Thanksgiving (1:8–10)

*⁸First, I thank my God through Jesus Christ for all of you,
because your faith is proclaimed in all the world. ⁹For God is my
witness, whom I serve with my Spirit in the gospel of his Son,
that without ceasing I mention you always in my prayers, ¹⁰ask-
ing that somehow by God's will I may now at last succeed in
coming to you.*

It was usual in ancient letters for thanksgiving to follow the
introductory greeting. The writer assured his reader of his grati-
tude to the gods and of his prayers for him. Paul's thanksgiving
in verse 8 has an almost liturgical form; we might compare the
structure of our present-day eucharistic prayers, thanksgiving to
God through Jesus Christ with a mention of the reason or cir-

cumstances. Paul here says "my God," adopting the prayer style of the psalms. The expression does not imply a privatization of the religious relationship to God but, like "my gospel," merely expresses Paul's intense consciousness of his mission. It is the same God who has called him and with whom he is linked by a special relationship, though one in which he can automatically include his readers; see 1:7: "God our Father."

Paul gives thanks for the Christian community in Rome, "for all of you." Even if he does not know them personally, or knows them only slightly, he does know their faith. Their faith has become famous "in all the world." The word that Paul uses to describe this fame ("proclaimed") connects it with preaching. The faith that the community has attained is saving faith, not simply because the believers reach salvation through faith, but also because the faith of the believers itself points to Jesus as the source of salvation. This faith is proclaimed through the believers or, rather, through their life of faith.

Verse 9 opens with an affirmation in which Paul once more mentions his special relationship with God. He calls on God to witness that he constantly remembers the Roman community in his prayers. God knows of his efforts to preach the gospel. In Paul's eyes this service of preaching is in the full sense "divine service" or worship. In 12:1 he uses the same word to describe the Christians' new "everyday" worship (see also Phil. 3:3). Paul performs his ministry of preaching, through which God's word reaches the Gentiles, as an act of worship to God. The phrase "in (or "with) my spirit" does not imply an interiorizing or spiritualizing of this worship. The clearest translation would be "with my whole being." Paul gives himself totally to God's service.

Purposes and Subject of the Letter (1:11–17)

[11]*For I long to see you, that I may impart to you some spiritual gift to strengthen you,* [12]*that is, that we may be mutually encouraged by each other's faith, both yours and mine.* [13]*I want you to know, brethren, that I have often intended to come to you (but*

thus far have been prevented), in order that I may reap some harvest among you as well as among the rest of the Gentiles. [14]I am under obligation both to Greeks and to barbarians, both to the wise and to the foolish: [15]so I am eager to preach the gospel to you also who are in Rome.

As an explanation of his wish to come to Rome, Paul says that he wishes to impart a " spiritual gift " to the community. What precisely this is, he leaves unspecified for the moment, but in verse 15 he says explicitly that he wishes to preach the gospel in Rome, and we shall hardly be wrong if we look in this direction for the spiritual gift that he wishes to impart. It is a gift of the power of the Spirit for the building up of the community. Paul assists in this by his preaching, though the assistance is not all on one side, indeed Paul the preacher hopes to be built up himself by the faith of the community. We should not see this as merely a tactful remark on Paul's part, made to avoid seeming too importunate to a community which still hardly knows him; in his missionary preaching Paul regards himself as always a recipient as well. The relationship between apostle and community is one of communication.

Paul's real intention, as we have seen, is to " reap some harvest " (1 : 13) in Rome as well as among the other Gentile nations. This gives us an indication of his future missionary plans. He wants now to move on to Rome because it is part of his missionary task. He is " under obligation " (1 : 14) to all alike, whatever their origin or education or their attitude to his preaching. He has no choice about whether or not to go to Rome; he is bound by the inexorable claim of the gospel, to which he has given himself totally. It is clear that Paul is not announcing a private visit, but the next stage in his missionary plans, which includes not just Rome but the whole of the western Empire (cf. 15 : 24). On this journey he wants to preach the gospel in the Roman community, not because they do not yet believe, but in order to win support for his plans among the Christians of Rome so that he can use this community as a base for an advance into the still unfamiliar parts of the Gentile world.

[16]For I am not ashamed of the gospel: it is the power of God for salvation to everyone who has faith, to the Jew first and also to the Greek. [17]For in it the righteousness of God is revealed through faith for faith; as it is written, " The righteous shall live by faith."

Paul has just mentioned his desire to extend his preaching of the gospel to Rome, and now, in verses 16–17, he begins the preaching; that is the significance of the summary of the main points of his gospel in these two verses. From other parts of the letter too it is clear that he means to set forth the gospel immediately, without waiting until he has reached Rome. His language is terse and emphatic. The various components of verses 16–17 are arranged around the word " gospel." The individual statements explain what Paul means by " gospel ": " it is the power of God . . . for in it the righteousness of God is revealed . . ." This list of the key terms of Paul's gospel defines the principal theme of the letter as a whole.

Why does Paul explicitly mention that he is *not ashamed of the gospel*? What reason could he have for being ashamed? Were there people in the Roman community who were ashamed of the gospel? From Paul's emphasis on the " power " of the gospel, it is likely that the reason for such a failure of appreciation or even for shame lies in the gospel itself. We should remember 1 Cor. 1:18, where the gospel is described as " the word of the cross," to those who are perishing, folly, but to those who are being saved, the power of God. This is a description of the crisis the gospel brings about. The cause is not its content, the " word of the cross," nor its preaching nor its preacher, but the power of God's revealing word, which provokes men either to acceptance or rejection. It was the same " Greeks " and " wise " (1:14) who had already had to be warned against resentment of a gospel which is no more than a message about a crucified saviour. In the sight of men the gospel is weak and helpless, but in the sight of God it is power and might to save. Paul has committed himself to what is from a human point of view a hopeless task, the complete accomplishment of God's purpose for man. Nevertheless he perseveres and is a fool in the eyes of the world: " We are fools for Christ's sake, but you are wise in Christ. We are weak, but you are strong. You are held in honor, but we in disrepute " (1 Cor. 4:10). Paul presents his gospel as God's work and not human wisdom. Men have to be ready to listen as well as to believe. This is what Paul asks the Romans to do now, as he prepares to proclaim to them the message of God's deeds.

It is by arousing faith in men that the gospel shows itself to be part of the process of salvation, God's powerful act to release mankind from its imprisonment in sin. The gospel announcement of God's saving activity makes this act of God present in history for man's salvation. In faith man experiences salvation as his new relationship to God. Paul regards faith, not as a condition to be fulfilled by men before they reach salvation, but as the way by which they participate now in God's eschatological saving act. That is why he is sure that all men are called to salvation. The universality of salvation is a necessary consequence of his gospel. The Jews take precedence in the history of salvation (" to the Jew first "), but now all, Jews and Gentiles, are called in the same way by the gospel. In Jesus Christ all previous claims to salvation are now revealed as provisional and also made worthless. From now on salvation comes to all only as a gift and only through faith.

" God's righteousness " means that in the process of salvation which Paul is proclaiming the decisive activity is God's. This is now confirmed independently by a quotation from Scripture. Only God can give faith in Jesus Christ such decisive importance for salvation, and therefore Paul refers back to God's promise as found in Hab. 2:4b: " The righteous shall live by faith." This is an argument from the history of the promise, designed to make clear that the ultimate basis of the Christ-event is God. In the preaching of the gospel and the faith of the believers in the present God is vindicated.

THE GOSPEL REVEALS THE RIGHTEOUSNESS OF GOD

(1:18—4:25)

In 1:15-17 we saw that Paul's main interest was the preaching of the gospel, and, more particularly, of the coming of salvation. These themes are developed in the section which follows, from two points of view.

(1) The gospel makes mankind aware of its true situation: as sinful mankind it is the object of the *wrath of God* (1:18—3:20).

(2) The gospel at the same time makes salvation available to all mankind by announcing it as a gift which can come only from God (3:21—4:25).

The two lines of thought connect and form a single argument.

The Wrath of God Revealed Against All Sin (1:18—3:20)

The wickedness of men

18*For the wrath of God is revealed from heaven against all ungodliness and wickedness of men who by their wickedness suppress the truth.*

Notice that this verse is a formal parallel to the previous one. The parallel is between the two revelations, of God's righteousness and of his wrathful judgment, a first indication that the wrath of God will turn out to be the other side of his righteousness. The wrath of God against the sin of mankind, which is the subject of this section, is nevertheless clearly subordinate to the subject announced in verse 17, which is in fact the subject of the gospel as a whole: "The righteousness of God is revealed." Starting from the gospel, Paul first goes back into the past of mankind and invites his readers to recognize themselves in his picture of their miserable history without salvation. The preaching of God's wrathful judgment is only one side of the saving revelation of God in the gospel, and only intelligible in the light of the full gospel. The wrathful judgment of God, like the gospel preaching, takes place in the presence of the listeners. What Paul is doing is part of his commission to preach: he reveals the true situation of mankind and places it under the judgment of God.

The wrath of God is directed at all the wickedness of men. In the light of God's saving revelation in the gospel man's sinfulness appears in its own "truth," as men's "godlessness" and "unrighteousness." Men are not "godless" only when they call themselves atheists. The godlessness Paul refers to is more basic. To say that a man is without God means that he is without the *living* God; the existence of godless men is an existence for death. The influence of death on men is shown in their behavior, and principally in their abandonment of God. Their godlessness is also unrighteousness because their abandonment of God also turns justice upside down. If we ask which justice, the justice of men or the justice of God, the answer is both. The justice of men is also the justice of God; when men act justly God too is justified. The justice of men has its ultimate foundation in God. This verse emphasizes particularly the circumstances of the overthrow of justice: men suppress "the truth," the truth of human existence, which includes the truth about man's existence with other men. This truth against which men rebel is in the end the personal truth of the living God himself. He reveals himself as the living God here and now in the gospel, in the revelation by the gospel of his truth as the final judgment which man cannot evade.

[19]*For what can be known about God is plain to them, because God has shown it to them.* [20]*Ever since the creation of the world his invisible nature, namely, his eternal power and deity, has been*

clearly perceived in the things that have been made. So they are
without excuse.

Paul now tries to give a justification of the wrath of God which
he has announced, and the attempt widens the scope of his argument. He reminds his readers of what is " obvious," of the general awareness of God among men. The assumption behind all
this is the revelation of the creator in his works. The " invisible "
nature of God, " his eternal power and deity," can be known
from his creation. Paul's thinking here, and his choice of words,
show the influence of the Hellenistic spirituality of his time; this
shows in his reference to the characteristics of God, his " eternal "
power and divine being—when Old Testament thought considered the eternity of God, it was usually from the point of
view of his faithfulness to his covenant with his people, and it
may be significant that the Greek word used here for " eternal "
only occurs once more in the New Testament, in Jude 6. But
this does not mean that Paul has simply taken over Greek ideas
about God; the mention of creation indicates a background for
Paul's preaching in Old Testament Judaism, and it is probably
from here that the influence of Greek thought is to be derived
(cf. Wis. 13 : 1–9).

Paul does not discuss in detail in this passage the problem of
" natural knowledge " of God; his main concern is to demonstrate man's lack of excuse. This is the significance of the fact
that God has been made known, through his own revelation of
himself as creator in his creation, but that this revelation has not
brought men to acknowledge the " truth," their true relationship to their creator. This original revelation of God now turns
into a burden of guilt for men.

[21]*For although they knew God they did not honor him as God or
give thanks to him, but they became futile in their thinking and
their senseless minds were darkened.* [22]*Claiming to be wise, they
became fools,* [23]*and exchanged the glory of the immortal God for
images resembling mortal man or birds or animals or reptiles.*

25

No man has an excuse before God. Paul now gives another, more specific, justification of this statement: men knew God but they did not honor him; they turned the worship of God into the worship of idols.

Knowledge of God should lead to correct worship of God. Glorifying and giving thanks to God is the obvious way for man to express his humanity before God: he owes himself to God. But the actual situation is very different. By their behavior men show themselves to be ungrateful. Even when they appear "wise," all their wisdom never penetrates to the true situation. They are blinded, their minds are darkened, they have become fools. They show this by their "worship of images." Here Paul obviously has in mind particular forms of pagan religious practice, but his attitude is not that of the history of culture or the history of religions—for him these are culpable perversions of the truth. The "worship of images" means simply the deification of created things. On this interpretation pagan religions are not some sort of preliminary stage in the development of true religion, nor degenerate or inadequate forms of a true relationship between God and men, but the perversion of these things. It is a sign of this folly of the wise that men ignore the "glory of the immortal God" and "squander" it. "Glory" is the way in which God the creator shows himself to his creation; the glory of God is the source of all life and purpose. As a substitute for this men have been satisfied with images of their own mortality: men, birds, animals, reptiles. Now they expect these substitutes to give them life.

[24]*Therefore God gave them up in the lusts of their hearts to impurity, to the dishonoring of their bodies among themselves, [25]because they exchanged the truth about God for a lie and worshipped and served the creature rather than the Creator, who is blessed for ever! Amen.*

It is not surprising that "impurity" and "the dishonoring of their bodies" should appear in the list of faults along with the worship of images, which was mentioned earlier. Idol worship and perversion of the moral order, particularly through sexual license, were commonly seen as linked in Jewish thought; moral perversion was seen as a natural result of idol worship (cf. Wis. 14:22–31). This situation, to Jewish eyes so typical of paganism, was ridiculed principally for apologetic reasons in order to emphasize the contrast with the Old Testament Judaism's faith in God and the moral behavior of the "righteous."

Paul does not take up this connection directly, but points first to mankind's guilt as something following from their perversion of "the truth about God." All other moral failings follow from this. Man's obstinate rejection of God also leads to further guilt and, by bringing man deeper into sin, shows that it falls under the wrathful judgment of God.

Man's fundamental sin is his rejection of the "truth about God." In this truth men were meant to find the truth about themselves by recognizing their true creator, but instead they have dared to replace him with creatures.

26For this reason God gave them up to dishonorable passions. Their women exchanged natural relations for unnatural, 27and their men likewise gave up natural relations with women and were consumed with passion for one another, men committing shameless acts with men and receiving in their own persons the due penalty for their error.

The beginning of this section repeats the beginning of verse 24, to give even greater force to the condemnation of man's perversion of creation. Now Paul fills in the picture of perversion in terms of man's unrestrained sexual desires.

It is no accident that Paul takes sexual licentiousness as his example of man's moral depravity. He would have had no lack of evidence in his time, and he is interpreting it here so as to support his preaching. His judgment on the abuses he describes has to be understood in the light of the assumptions prevalent in his age and culture. The apostle's Hellenistically educated contemporaries were familiar with the demands of morality, which they derived from a moral law analogous to the natural law. And yet the demand to live according to nature always seemed to have room for an individualistic striving after whatever happiness could be attained, including sexual pleasure in a more or less sublimated form. Excesses did provoke criticism, it is true, but this never went beyond ideas of nature. In contrast, Paul's judgment is based on an idea of creation. He uses the language of the Jewish apologetic critique of pagan practices, but his basic attitude to them is not an ethical one. They point to man's fundamental sin; he has forgotten that creator and creature are not interchangeable. But the creator has now revealed himself to God-forsaken man by giving him up to his passions so that he feels the " due penalty " in the workings of his irrational impulses. Paul sees the " wrath of God " already at work in the history of mankind. In the present, in the preaching of the gospel, the " wrath of God " is revealed in its eschatological finality.

[28]*And since they did not see fit to acknowledge God, God gave them up to a base mind and to improper conduct.* [29]*They were filled with all manner of wickedness, evil, covetousness, malice. Full of envy, murder, strife, deceit, malignity, they are gossips,* [30]*slanderers, haters of God, insolent, haughty, boastful, inventors of evil, disobedient to parents,* [31]*foolish, faithless, heartless, ruthless.*

Once more Paul refers to man's fundamental refusal, the root of his defective relationship with God. Although they knew God (v. 21), men denied him his due honor as creator. They have deliberately abandoned their fundamental contact with life—this is what " knowledge of God " means.

God's activity as man's judge now affects all man's behavior. In this light all mankind necessarily appears as an abandoned race. This is the meaning of the " catalogue of vices " which Paul inserts here; such lists were to some extent commonplaces in ancient ethical writings such as those of the Stoics, and Paul's list probably derives from similar passages in Jewish writings influenced by the Stoics, such as Wis. 14:22-26; 4 Mac. 1-3. Whereas in the preceding verses he gave detailed examples of unnatural sexuality, here he contents himself with a list of wrong attitudes and actions. They are the hidden working out of God's judgment, which is what Paul wants to show. This is why he does not ask whether man only does evil or whether good cannot also be found in his actions. Since he is not interested here in ethical questions for their own sake, and does not want to examine the theoretical possibility of a morally good life, this passage provides no answer to that question. This is not because of any inadequacy in Paul's approach but because in the light of the Pauline kerygma such a question is irrelevant. Behind Paul's words here is the " truth about God," which says of the situation of the whole of mankind that before God all men are sinners. All men must admit this, and when it is admitted there is no longer any point in asking how great a sinner a man is.

Looked at in this way, the twenty-one items in this list of human sins need not detain us. Paul at any rate was not interested here in an accurate description of the morals and customs of his time.

32Though they know God's decree that those who do such things deserve to die, they not only do them but approve those who practise them.

In conclusion Paul adds a final twist to his charge. All those who know of the demands of God's justice, who sin in the knowledge of the death sentence, act in this way in spite of it; not only do they do this themselves, but they also share the mentality of all who act in this way. This secret or open conspiracy against the creator is the final expression of the guilt of all mankind. There is no excuse or exemption for anything in Paul's list; everything deserves punishment.

The Particular Sin of the Jews (2:1—3:20)

The previous section, 1:18-32, often seemed particularly concerned with the sins of the Gentiles. This impression is due mainly to Paul's use in his argument of the language of the contemporary Jewish critique of the Gentile world and its corruption, although Paul never explicitly subscribes himself to the Jewish interpretation. But even if Paul had the image of the vice-ridden Gentile world foremost in his mind when he composed this description of human sinfulness, nevertheless the thrust of his argument as a whole is towards establishing the guilt of all men before God.

In order to avoid giving the impression that the Jews were excluded from this picture of sinful mankind, and were better placed to face God's wrathful judgment than the Gentiles, Paul now addresses himself specifically to Jewish self-righteousness. In the light of the gospel this appears as the characteristic sin of the Jews, though the Jew here addressed by Paul is not to be regarded simply as the representative of a particular race, but as the type of mankind as a whole in its attempts to present pleas of mitigation in the face of God's judgment.

Paul's argument divides into five parts, which finally converge on a single point: "None is righteous, no, not one " (3:10).

The Judgment of God on the Man who Presumes to Judge Others (2:1-16)

¹Therefore you have no excuse, O man, whoever you are, when you judge another; for in passing judgment upon him you condemn yourself, because you, the judge, are doing the very same things. ²We know that the judgment of God rightly falls on those who do such things.

Paul speaks directly to "man," and confronts him with his essential characteristic: "you judge." Since general sinfulness in the passage just preceding was given "Gentile" features, the natural interpretation here would be to see the man who judges as the Jew and the "other," whom he judges, as the Gentile. And it is in fact clear that Paul has the Jew in mind here, even though he doesn't say so explicitly. The Jew is par excellence the type of the man who judges others, and it is this self-righteous Jew whom Paul now accuses. The Jew believes that the charges of idolatry and unnatural sexual practices do not apply to him, at least not to the same extent, but for all his condemnation of such behavior he is no better than the man who does such things.

The Jew might pride himself on his closer knowledge of God than the Gentile, in language like that of Wis. 15:1: "But thou, O God, art gracious and true," and "Neither did the mischievous invention of man deceive us, nor an image spotted with divers colors, the painter's fruitless labor" (Wis. 15:4). It cannot be said that the Jew was not aware of his sins; he was, but he also knew that they were finally taken up into the "compassion" and "mercy" of God: "For if we sin, we are thine, knowing thy power: but we will not sin, knowing that we are counted thine" (Wis. 15:2). There is no reason to doubt that this pious Jew's confession is genuine, a genuine expression of religion, and yet it is this confession which sounds through the boast of the Pharisee in Lk. 18:11: "God, I thank thee that I am not like other men, extortioners, unjust adulterers . . ."

³Do you suppose, O man, that when you judge those who do such things and yet do them yourself, that you will escape the judgment of God? ⁴Or do you presume upon the riches of his kindness and forbearance and patience? Do you not know that God's kindness is meant to lead you to repentance? ⁵But by your hard and impenitent heart you are storing up wrath for yourself on the day of wrath when God's righteous judgment will be revealed.

Paul wants to reveal to the Jew his true situation, that he is *not* righteous and will not escape the judgment of God. In verse 4 he begins to argue once more that the Jew's trust in God's goodness, forbearance and patience is *presumption,* because he does not allow God's goodness to lead him to repentance.

What does repentance involve? A return to the covenant and commandments of God? Since Paul is describing the sinfulness of both Jews and the rest of mankind from the standpoint of the gospel, " God's goodness " must be understood as leading, not to a return to a renewed form of the old covenant, but to the decisive, eschatological turning in faith to Christ. The Jews, however, have met God's eschatological offer of salvation in Christ with hard and impenitent hearts.

This is the real sin of the Jews, which Paul sees exemplified many times in the history of the infidelity of God's people to the covenant. By her repeated breaches of the covenant Israel had already shown the hardness of her heart towards the promises of God, which were part of the revelation of his righteousness. In the light of the gospel it becomes clear that Israel's obstinate resistance to the promises of God reached its culmination in her resistance to the gospel. This sin is the basic reason for God's wrath against Israel on the " day of wrath " (cf. 1:18 and 2:6).

⁶For he will render to every man according to his works: ⁷to those who by patience in well-doing seek for glory and honor and immortality, he will give eternal life; ⁸but for those who are factious and do not obey the truth, but obey wickedness, there will be wrath and fury. ⁹There will be tribulation and distress for every human being who does evil, the Jew first and also the Greek, ¹⁰but glory and honor and peace for every one who does good, the Jew first and also the Greek.

God's judgment has one standard for all, and Paul describes it in the words of Ps. 62:12: " He will render to every man according to his works." The important point of the scriptural quotation is not the proclamation of God's impartial principle of retribution so much as the statement that all men are subject to the one judgment of God. All men know the standard; they know that the criterion is doing the works of God, and that on this basis each man may look forward either to " eternal life " or " wrath and fury." It is this general awareness and its related expectations to which Paul is appealing here, repeating, evidently for the sake of emphasis, the contrast between those who do good and those who do evil (verses 9–10). Paul introduces judgment according to works here, not simply to recall an ideal principle, but in order to emphasize, through the contrast between " eternal life," " glory," " honor " and " peace " on the one hand, and " wrath and fury," " tribulation " and " distress " on the other, the failings of all who stand under the judgment of God.

We should remember in reading these verses that Paul has the Jews particularly in mind. The phrases used here acquire their full significance in the context of the early Christian missionaries' experience with the Jews. It was the Jews who showed themselves as " factious," obstinate, the sort of people who refused the obedience of faith to the truth of the gospel. As a result they, even more than the Gentiles, are the object of God's wrath.

¹¹*For God shows no partiality.*

Paul's thesis throughout this passage has been that all men are sinners and all need God's salvation. In support of this he emphasizes in verse 11 the universal application of God's actions in order to refute yet again all Jewish claims based on salvation history. This connects with verses 1–3: the Jew is no better off than the Gentile. Nevertheless there remains a tension between the priority of the Jews in salvation history and the universality of sin, and this cannot be reduced. This tension forces us, like Paul, to accept that God's eschatological activity in the gospel does not mean that he disregards human history, but, on the contrary, that he subjects all men's historically acquired characteristics to judgment.

¹²All who have sinned without the law will also perish without the law, and all who have sinned under the law will be judged by the law. ¹³For it is not the hearers of the law who are righteous before God, but the doers of the law who will be justified.

Verses 12 and 13 assert once more the universality of judgment, this time with reference to the Jews' obstinate reliance on their law. No partiality towards persons also means no partiality towards the law. The law is no protection against judgment. Therefore the Gentiles, who were without the law and sinned as a result, perish without the law—here Paul can agree with the Jews, though from a different viewpoint. But the Jews too, who have the law and therefore understand God's plans, will be judged, that is, condemned, by the law. Because, Paul explains, it is not the hearers of the law who are righteous before God, but the " doers of the law " who will be justified.

This is the first time in the Epistle to the Romans that Paul uses the term " justify ". It is clear from the context that it is legal language, and this will be important for our understanding of the terms in its future uses.

¹⁴When Gentiles who have not the law do by nature what the law requires, they are a law to themselves, even though they do not have the law. ¹⁵They show that what the law requires is written on their hearts, while their conscience also bears witness and their conflicting thoughts accuse or perhaps excuse them ¹⁶on that day when, according to my gospel, God judges the secrets of men by Christ Jesus.

In the face of God's judgment the previous distinction between Jew and Gentile is softened. Paul now shows in verses 14–15

34

that even the possession of the law allows only a relative distinction between Jew and Gentile. These verses are strictly a digression from the main point of the passage, the sinfulness of the Jews. When the Gentiles who do not have the law do by nature what the law requires, this shows that they, although they do not have the law, are a law to themselves. And verse 15 explains: they show that what the law requires is written on their hearts. There is no need to go into the question whether only some of the Gentiles are meant or the Gentiles in general, or whether those meant follow all the prescriptions of the Mosaic law. Paul's main point is to soften the distinction between Jew and Gentile.

The Gentiles do " by nature " what the law requires. This corresponds to what is said in verse 15 about the requirements of the law being written on their hearts. Paul is referring here, as in 1:19-20, to the inner unity between the creature and his creator. The fact of creation enables the Gentiles to do the good which the law positively enjoins. It is remarkable that Paul says here that they in fact do it, but evidently it makes no difference to the general sinfulness of the Gentiles.

Finally Paul comes back to the idea of judgment on the Jews which he introduced in 2:5 in order once more to place Jews and Gentiles together under the judgment of God. " That day " on which judgment is passed, the " day of wrath " (2:5), is the final day, when human activity comes to an end and a reckoning is made of every action. For Paul " that day " is no longer a time to be awaited in a distant future, but the end which already reaches into the present. The events of the end have already begun in Jesus Christ, and in 1:18 we learn that it is impossible to separate God's wrathful judgment from the eschatological events which are shaping the present and relegate it to a remote future. This is confirmed by Paul's words in 2:16, " according to my gospel, God judges . . . by Christ Jesus," judgment is already taking place in the present. This is the opening announcement of Paul's gospel: the history of mankind, in all its forms, stands under the judgment of God.

[17]But if you call yourself a Jew and rely upon the law and boast of your relation to God [18]and know his will and approve what is excellent, because you are instructed in the law, [19]and if you are sure that you are a guide to the blind, a light to those who are in darkness, [20]a corrector of the foolish, a teacher of children, having in the law the embodiment of knowledge and truth.

Paul continues his attack on the Jew, and more particularly on his claims to advantage. There can, however, be seen in the whole passage an effort not simply to score off the Jew and crush him with a mass of accusations. Paul's view of the situation of the Jews is more subtle than that, and he clearly has in mind all the time the priority of Jew over Gentile which is an undeniable feature of salvation history.

The catalogue begins with a direct address to the Jew, who emphatically calls himself " Jew," a title which involved specific claims. Paul at first leaves the Jew undisturbed in his view of himself, without irony, but he will later use it to trap the Jew firmly in his real guilt. The Jew's main title of honor is the law. Everything else in verses 17–20 is an expansion of this basic statement. In his possession of the law the Jew is sure of God. He glories " in God " almost as a matter of course, since in the law he has in his hands the deeds of God's covenant. Through the law he knows the will of God and can therefore judge what is important. As a person who knows the will of God through the law, he cannot be taken unawares by the vicissitudes of life.

In verse 19 there is a shift of emphasis. The list of Jewish distinctions now begins to concentrate on those to whom the Jews have responsibilities, the Gentiles. This presupposes that all that the Jew claims is not meant for him alone but also for those who do not possess these advantages. The Jew is also aware of this, which is why he tries to win Gentiles for the law and make proselytes. The four characterizations listed in 2:19 describe in formal language the claims of the Jew to leadership: he considers himself a guide to the blind, a light in darkness, a corrector of the foolish and a teacher of children. Paul is here drawing on Jewish tradition, and making the same use of it as Jesus in the saying quoted in Mt. 15:14, where he says of the Pharisees, "They are blind guides." When the "guides to the blind" can themselves be described as blind, the situation of Israel is obviously serious.

The only ground the Jew has for such claims is the statement that, as verse 20b puts it, he has "in the law the embodiment of knowledge and truth." In this verse Paul picks out the crown of the whole list of Jewish advantages. As in verse 17, at the beginning, so again in verse 20, at the end of this elaborate structure of clauses, stands the law, the expression of Jewish consciousness. Paul has turned the list of claims and boasts right round, so that instead of confirming the Jew in his privileged position it emphasizes his lack of excuse.

[21]*You then who teach others, will you not teach yourself? While you preach against stealing, do you not steal?* [22]*You who say that one must not commit adultery, do you commit adultery? You who abhor idols, do you rob temples?* [23]*You who boast in the law, do you dishonor God by breaking the law?* [24]*For, as it is written, "The name of God is blasphemed among the Gentiles because of you."*

In verse 21 Paul begins again, "you then who teach others..." In these verses he takes up key terms of the preceding boast in order to make a *reductio ad absurdum* of the Jew's claims. "You who teach others, will you not teach yourself?" Paul's aim now becomes immediately clear, to expose the self-righteousness of the Jew and so destroy his claim. Three more sentences follow in the same style. Each of the three questions mentions a serious sin, even a crime. You preach against stealing and you steal; you condemn adultery and you commit adultery; you abhor idols and you rob temples. The last is a particularly serious offense. There could be various motives which would lead a Jew to rob a pagan temple, but Paul is only interested here in showing that the abomination the Jew sees in idols is reproduced in his own abominable actions and attitudes.

Verse 23 sums everything up. The key phrase is "break the law." There is a contradiction between the Jewish boast, based on possession of the law, and the Jew's actual behavior which can be bluntly described as breaking the law. It now becomes clear what is ultimately involved in the Jew's guilt: he dishonors God, that is, he fails to keep the first and most important commandment of the decalogue, to allow God to be completely God.

The name of God is despised among the Gentiles. Paul ends with a scriptural text (Is. 52:5) to support his argument. The Jews' own view of themselves and their mission told them that their behavior was meant to lead the Gentiles to acknowledge God. Now the opposite has happened: the behavior of the Jews is the reason for the blaspheming of God by the Gentiles.

25Circumcision indeed is of value if you obey the law; but if you break the law your circumcision becomes uncircumcision. 26So, if a man who is uncircumcised keeps the precepts of the law, will not his uncircumcision be regarded as circumcision? 27Then those who are physically uncircumcised but keep the law will condemn you who have the written code and circumcision but break the law.

Paul begins as though he were taking part in a discussion about circumcision: "As regards circumcision, it is only of value if you keep the law." His statement implies a fundamental connection between law and circumcision. It is an argument he has used before, in the Epistle to the Galatians; according to Gal. 3:3 everyone who receives circumcision is bound to keep the whole law. The view that circumcision was only of value if a man kept the law " would have been rejected by rabbinic scholars; for them circumcision in itself had power to save every Israelite from the fire of Gehenna and make him a son of the future world " (Strack-Billerbeck, *Kommentar zum Neuen Testament aus Talmud und Midrasch* III, 119).

Paul's aim is to undermine the Jew's false assurance of salvation, and he now goes a step further by taking up the contrast with the Gentiles from 2:12–15. In that passage he had been able to credit the Gentiles, those born without the law, with a degree of achievement in keeping the law; they showed that they had the demands of the law written in their hearts (2:15). But if the uncircumcised in fact keep the precepts of the law (2:26) does not all that makes circumcision a title of honor apply also to the uncircumcised? Paul probably has in mind the promises attached to circumcision. His love of paradoxes leads him to a perhaps rather loaded conclusion : their uncircumcision will be regarded as circumcision.

So according to 2:27, the Gentiles, uncircumcised "by nature," who keep the law will finally through their keeping of the law judge the Jews, who though they have the written code and circumcision have been found to be breakers of the law. The relationship between Jew and Gentile implied in 2:1 is now completely reversed. We find a parallel from the gospels in Mt. 12:41 (=Lk. 11:32; Q): "The men of Nineveh will arise at the judgment with this generation and condemn it."

28For he is not a real Jew who is one outwardly, nor is true circumcision something external and physical. 29He is a real Jew who is one inwardly, and real circumcision is a matter of the heart, spiritual and not literal. His praise is not from men but from God.

Verses 28–29 offer a general conclusion from the whole of the previous argument. The subject is the " real Jew." The real

"Jew" is not the man who is one for all to see, but the man who is one inwardly. Paul derives this judgment from the earlier contrast between circumcision and uncircumcision, and so adds a parallel clause: real circumcision is not that which is displayed in the flesh, externally, but "a matter of the heart."

In the light of the preceding argument this conclusion is surprising. One might have expected the chapter to end with a condemnation of the Jew, since it had been established that he was no better than the Gentile. One might have expected a conclusion in terms of universal sinfulness, which after all is Paul's main theme. But instead we have a contrast between the true and false Jew.

Does the idea of a "real Jew" make sense in the time before Christ and under sin? It is clear that with the question of the "real Jew" Paul has gone beyond the limits of the previous discussion. He deliberately allows his exposition of universal sinfulness to be interrupted by an anticipatory reference to the new "order" of belonging to Christ, in which "circumcision of the heart" becomes a reality.

"Circumcision of the heart" is a phrase used by the Old Testament prophets. In Ezek. 44:7, 9 the idea remains within the narrow conception of Judaism: "uncircumcised in heart" and "uncircumcised in flesh" are here still identical. A critical note can be heard in Jer. 4:4; 6:10; 9:25-26. "Circumcise yourselves to the LORD, remove the foreskins of your hearts" (4:4). "All these nations are uncircumcised, and all the house of Israel is uncircumcised in heart" (9:26). But even though the antithesis between merely external circumcision and circumcision of the heart is quite familiar to Old Testament Judaism, it nevertheless acquires a new meaning with Paul. In the polemic of Philippians 3 Paul exclaims, "We are the true circumcision, who worship God in spirit, and glory in Christ Jesus, and put no confidence in the flesh. Though I myself have reason for confidence in the flesh also." This text shows that Paul regards true circumcision as having become a reality in Christians.

¹Then what advantage has the Jew? Or what is the value of cir-cumcision? ²Much in every way. To begin with, the Jews are entrusted with the oracles of God. ³What if some were unfaith-ful? Does their faithlessness nullify the faithfulness of God? ⁴By no means! Let God be true though every man be false, as it is written, " That thou mayest be justified in thy words, and prevail when thou art judged."

Paul begins by taking up the question of the advantages of the Jew and the value of circumcision from the previous discussion, an indication that he cannot dismiss the priority of Jew over Gentile in salvation history as easily as might have appeared from chapter 2. Though all are equal before God (cf. 2:11), the Jew nevertheless retains an " objective " advantage, exemplified above all by the " oracles of God " entrusted to Israel. Paul respects this privileged position of Israel as against the Gentiles, but what is the significance of God's speaking to Israel in the past? Is the special choice of which Israel was the object an inalienable possession? Paul does not answer the question, and indeed he does not continue with his list of the advantages of Israel. His clear implication, however, is that even the " oracles of God " given to Israel in the past are invalidated by Israel's present failure to recognize the decisive word of God in the gospel as his communication of himself to all men.

The list of Jewish advantages begun in verse 2 is continued in 9:4 in another context, where Paul also discusses in more detail the special position of Israel.

Mention of the oracles of God leads Paul to the question of God's faithfulness to his promises. If it has been established that the Jews have been unfaithful by breaking the law (chapter 2), does their infidelity nullify the faithfulness of God? Paul says carefully, " if *some* were unfaithful." Is this meant as a limita-tion? The meaning cannot be that only some of the people of Israel sinned in the past, and the rest have incurred no guilt. It is helpful here to look at 11:25. There Paul says, "A hardening has come upon part of Israel," meaning a hardening against the eschatological offer of salvation in the gospel. His meaning in the present passage is the same when he says, "some were unfaithful": the "remnant are those who have given their obedience to the gospel in the present."

The factual connection between God's faithfulness and the faithlessness of Israel involves the Old Testament idea of the covenant. According to this the Jews' past actions in breaking the covenant could imply the release of God from his obligations as the other party. Paul rejects this view. What the situation shows is, rather, that God is true even if men are false, as Ps. 116:11 says. This thought is continued in a further Scripture text: "that thou mayest be justified in thy words and prevail when thou art judged" (Ps. 51:6). The implication is that Israel's offense against God in breaking the covenant is to be settled by a legal dispute. There can be no doubt about which side will win. God's victory is won in the revelation of his righteousness.

⁵But if our wickedness serves to show the justice of God, what shall we say? That God is unjust to inflict wrath on us? (I speak in a human way.) ⁶By no means! For then how could God judge the world? ⁷But if through my falsehood God's truthfulness abounds to his glory, why am I still being condemned as a sinner? ⁸And why not do evil so that good may come?—as some people slanderously charge us with saying. Their condemnation is just.

The infidelity of the Jews is being established in a legal action brought by God. The result of these proceedings is not simply to prove the guilt of the Jews and the innocence of God and his integrity, but also to demonstrate God's righteousness as shown in his saving will. In the premise of verse 5 the true meaning of the guilt of the Jews appears clearly. In the legal proceedings the Jew represents not just his own people but all mankind. In the face of God's righteousness all mankind's efforts simply demonstrate their own deep-rooted unrighteousness.

But Paul can also put this the other way round, as we see from verse 5. In contrast with God's righteousness not only is man's desire to be in the right nothing less than unrighteousness, but we can even say that man's unrighteousness manifests God's righteousness. This formulation is sufficiently misleading to give rise to the conclusion that the issue is putting God in the right. Or, in an even more extreme formulation, the important thing is that human wickedness reveals God's truth (verse 7), the extent of human sin reveals his grace (verse 8). Paul rejects these extreme consequences of his message of grace. The central theme of the proclamation of God's righteousness is the saving of the sinner who is lost in his wickedness. No rights derive to the sinner from God's rights: he cannot identify himself with his sinfulness and simply remain in his sin, cut off from God for ever. In dealing with these issues Paul carries on the metaphor of legal proceedings which began with the quotation from the psalms in verse 4. The main result of the man's argument—in verses 5-8 he is no longer just a Jew—is to demonstrate the hopelessness of a man who tries to cut himself off from God.

Paul's missionary preaching had obviously aroused objections such as the ones he quotes verbatim here. " Doesn't your preaching imply doing evil that good may come? Aren't you making the action of grace directly dependent on the doing of evil?" This is the motivation for the otherwise very peculiar questions in verses 5-7. They are sophisticated questions, but in quoting them Paul is thinking in advance of the familiar objections to his missionary preaching. He is here refuting an interpretation of his teaching on grace which would make it possible to do evil intentionally or to remain willingly under sin in order to let God's grace increase. The theme of Paul's whole argument is the hopelessness of man under sin. For the man who is redeemed from sin the new obedience to God is not only possible but a duty. Paul develops this point in detail in chapter 6.

43

*⁹What then? Are we Jews any better off? No, not at all; for I
have already charged that all men, both Jews and Greeks, are
under the power of sin, ¹⁰as it is written :*
    " none is righteous, no, not one;
¹¹no one understands, no one seeks for God.
¹²All have turned aside, together they have gone wrong;
    no one does good, no, not even one."
¹³"Their throat is an open grave,
they use their tongues to deceive."
    " The venom of asps is under their lips."
¹⁴"Their mouth is full of curses and bitterness."
¹⁵"Their feet are swift to shed blood,
¹⁶in their paths are ruin and misery,
¹⁷and the way of peace they do not know."
¹⁸"There is no fear of God before their eyes."

The question of the advantages of the Jew raised in verse 1 is
taken up again in verse 9, but only briefly, to be answered
with a negative which contrasts with verse 2. The contrast is
still remarkable, even if Paul's answer here does not amount to
a complete denial. Paul agrees that the Jews have precedence,
insofar as they are the bearers of the promise, but at the same
time he sees them included in the general sinfulness of man
and in the gospel of God's saving acts which is directed at all
men. Here in verse 9 Paul is dealing in the first place simply
with the general guilt of both Jews and Greeks. He now
draws the conclusions of his previous argument: Jews as well
as Greeks are guilty. In the preceding discussion, in 1:18—
3:10, Paul has accused all, which means that all are under
sin. This statement is the conclusion of Paul's whole exposition
of human wickedness. That mankind as a whole is under the
power of sin, which men have helped to power by their own
actions, is a final and conclusive argument for their need of
salvation.

A series of Scripture texts now drives home the point of sin's
control over man. Most of them are from the psalms, except

for verses 15-17, which come from Is. 59:7-8. A single thread runs through the quotations, the godlessness of men, and this collection of quotations, largely from the psalms, itself forms a psalm or, more precisely, a "complaint."

The scriptural quotations also make the point that it is God who is the accuser of mankind in 1:18—3:20. His accusing word is heard in the word of Scripture.

¹⁹Now we know that whatever the law says it speaks to those who are under the law, so that every mouth may be stopped, and the whole world may be held accountable to God.

Even if the collection of texts in 3:11–18 established the general guilt of all men, Paul nevertheless has the Jews particularly in mind. It is to the Jews that all this was said, "so that every mouth may be stopped." Paul has just shown in verses 1-8 that it is the Jews in particular who right to the end have objections to God's saving actions. The Scriptures (here described as "the law") brought the word of God to those "who are under the law," that is, the Jews, and "the law" in this respect is less of a boast than an indictment, reducing every discordant voice to silence, so that the whole world may be found guilty before God.

Conclusion: No Justification by Works of the Law (3:20)

²⁰For no human being will be justified in his sight by works of the law, since through the law comes knowledge of sin.

Paul here formulates a fundamental principle of his preaching This verse and the next together form the central statement of his message of justification.

In verse 20 Paul takes up the quotation from Ps. 143 used in verse 10, "No man living is righteous before thee," and applies this generalization of Old Testament piety to the hopeless situation of mankind before the gospel. This is rather different from the psalmist's original meaning. Among the Jews it was quite possible for the recognition of guilt and the consciousness of being a chosen people to exist side by side without requiring the confession of guilt to lead to a humiliating self-abasement. For Paul, however, such a co-existence between awareness of guilt and consciousness of election is no longer possible. It is precisely this Jewish consciousness, which shows itself in the boast about the possession of the law, which is ruled out. This is why he immediately adds, as a gloss on the psalm text, " by works of the law."

The " works of the law " demonstrate the powerlessness of the law. The law makes demands, but does not give itself the power to carry out its demands. This does not mean that it is impossible to fulfill the law, but that in practice it is not being fulfilled. Man is not justified by " works of the law " alone. Such an assertion must obviously hit a Jew in his most sensitive spot, his Jewishness. Paul is here attacking the Jewish claim to a special position in salvation history. Paul sees this special position as taken up into what has now become a positive possibility, justification by faith. On this see especially Gal. 2:16, where Paul developed his ideas on justification for the first time.

The Jew's question about the value of the law now at last has an answer: " Through the law comes knowledge of sin."

The Righteousness of God Manifested Through Faith in Jesus Christ (3:21—4:25)

It is striking that the Jew and his position in the debate on salvation should be dealt with so explicitly at this point, just before the passage in which the " positive " proclamation of salvation is made. In essence, the weight of the whole passage 1:18—3:20 is directed at the Jews, not the Gentiles. Evidently Paul considers it particularly necessary in dealing with the Roman Christian community to expose and demolish the Jewish position. In this process the " Jewish question " acquires exemplary status; it becomes the model with which Paul works out the general problem of salvation for all mankind. With their apparently assured claim on God, and their claim to possess the only true religion, the Jews must have seemed a particularly suitable object for Paul's gospel of grace.

This is confirmed by the transition from verse 20 to verse 21. The " positive " presentation of the message is sharply contrasted with the Jewish position: " But now the righteousness of God has been manifested *apart from law*." The case of the Jews is to make clear what the proclamation of God's saving activity means for all men. Paul's subject is not only God's initiative for the justification of the Jews, but his action for the justification of mankind as a whole, if they submit in faith to his saving action. And yet is it noteworthy that the case of the Jews is still the dominant model in Paul's exposition of the message of salvation in the passage which follows. The whole section is based on Jewish or Jewish-Christian ideas.

The Manifestation of the Righteousness of God (3:21–26)

[21]*But now the righteousness of God has been manifested apart from law, although the law and the prophets bear witness to it,* [22a]*the righteousness of God through faith in Jesus Christ for all who believe.*

" But now . . ." This is no timeless, supra-historical " now," but the decisive " now " of the present, the moment at which God's word reaches us. Paul's language makes it clear that when he speaks of the Christ-event he is not thinking of a moment in the past, but of the present in which the gospel is being preached and heard. It is in the gospel that the manifestation of God reaches men; the time of the gospel is the same as the time of Jesus Christ and his saving act. The present, in which Jesus Christ is proclaimed as the salvation of the whole world, is the decisive moment for salvation—though this of course does not mean that the salvation which is here proclaimed as a present event does not depend on the unique event of Christ, his death and resurrection.

"But now . . ." The news of salvation reaches man in the depths of his guilt. On man's part the gospel demands no preparation other than that he should let himself be found by God in his need for redemption.

The Christ-event is the manifestation of God's righteousness. This is the deepest dimension of Jesus' death and resurrection as saving events. In Jesus' gift of his life for men "God's righteousness" is revealed. This phrase describes the fact that in Jesus' work God was acting for the salvation of man. What man experiences in his meeting with the dying and rising Lord is the action of God, the God who has drawn near in Jesus. In this context God's "righteousness" cannot be understood in the usual Western meaning of the term. "God's righteousness" is not the ethical idea that God is righteous (just), but says that he is in the right *vis-à-vis* guilty mankind and that his dealings with mankind are right (justified), so that what is God's right becomes right for man. The manifestation of God calls men to acknowledge the justice of God's cause, and in the process man discovers what it means to be just in the sight of God. All this takes place "now," in Jesus Christ, in whom God is made manifest. The gospel, by which "God's righteousness" is made manifest, proclaims the power made available to men in the death and resurrection of Jesus.

[22b]*For there is no distinction;* [23]*since all have sinned and fall short of the glory of God,* [24]*they are justified by his grace as a gift, through the redemption which is in Christ Jesus.*

Once more Paul stresses the universal effect of the Christ-event and faith, by means of a reference back to the statements of 1 : 18—3 : 20. All are affected both by sin and now by the Christ-event. *There is no distinction*: all have sinned, all are in need of redemption, all are addressed by God in Jesus Christ, all have access to God in faith. Paul's insistence yet again that there is no distinction is a further indication that his argument is largely directed at the Jews. It is the Jew in particular who must renounce his privileges in order to share in the new way of being in relation to God, which through faith in Jesus Christ can now be seen to be the only way of being in relation to God.

All are addressed by God, since " all . . . fall short of the glory of God." Here we catch sight of another meaning of " God's righteousnes," sharing in God's glory. This share is lost to man as a result of sin but restored to the sinner in the form of justification (cf. 8:30; 2 Cor. 3:18), though for the justified it still remains both an acquisition and a blessing to look forward to (cf. 5:2; 8:18).

After the declaration of sin—rather abruptly—comes the declaration of justification. These are two elements of an antithesis, though Paul does not particularly emphasize the contrast here. The process of justification is given a clearer Christological basis than in 3:21-22: the justification of the men who sinned takes place through the " grace " which is at work in the " redemption which is in Christ Jesus." The emphasis on the gratuitous character of justification corresponds to " apart from law " and the denial of efficacy to works of the law in verses 21 and 20. The process of redemption established by the death of Jesus is further explained in the next verse.

[25]*whom God put forward as an expiation by his blood, to be received by faith. This was to show God's righteousness, because in his divine forbearance he had passed over former sins;* [26]*it was to prove at the present time that he himself is righteous and that he justifies him who has faith in Jesus.*

God brings about " redemption " (verse 24) in and through Jesus Christ, whom he " put forward as an expiation . . ." The reference here is to the expiation made by Jesus' sacrifice of his life, an expiation for the sins of men. There is no need

49

here to develop the idea of expiation beyond Paul's brief mention of it, and it would certainly be wrong to read into this sentence an expiation theology which portrayed God as demanding and receiving expiation, and the bloody death of Jesus as the expiatory sacrifice offered in our place to placate God. The crucial point is that what Jesus achieves by laying down his life is the work of God himself. God does not demand expiation, he guarantees it; that is what this passage is really saying about expiation.

God took the first step, without waiting for men to bring him the required expiatory offering. He himself brings about expiation and thereby redemption from sins. At the end of verse 25 is a reference to God's wish for the success of redemption. The whole work of redemption is accomplished " because he had passed over former sins." The sins committed before the decisive events of salvation are, for the Jewish Christians, whose attitudes clearly lie behind this terminology, the sins committed in the former covenant with God. The background to this argument is God's covenant relationship with Israel. Through Jesus Christ's sacrifice of his life the covenant relationship with God is repaired and ratified again.

Justification by Faith Alone the Basis of the Unity of Jews and Gentiles in One Church (3:27–31)

27Then what becomes of our boasting? It is excluded. On what principle? On the principle of works? No, but on the principle of faith. 28For we hold that a man is justified by faith apart from works of law.

In the previous paragraph Paul has set out his message of justification in very concentrated theological terms. Now he brings the Jews once more face to face with their boast. What has happened to your boast in the law now, after God's eschatological saving act? What happens to your advantages if everything depends on Jesus? Every claim on God is excluded by the Christ-event. The Jews based their blasphemous self-assertion on the Mosaic law and on "works of the law," and now Paul says of these "works" that God does not take them into account in justification. We need to see this connection in order to give verse 28 its proper significance as a restatement of what Paul has already argued in detail in verses 21–26. That men are justified by faith is not, of course, something one discovers for oneself, but only through contact with the Christ-event. This is what is behind the "we hold" of verse 28 (cf. Gal. 2:16: "we who . . . know"); the words have the tone of a formal statement of faith.

The translation "by faith alone" is justified on linguistic grounds, but it should not be given the polemical overtones it acquired during the Reformation. Paul's intention is not to emphasize a principle of faith as opposed to a principle of works, but to make it clear that the works of the law are excluded. It is clear from his advice and exhortation in other contexts that he does not dispute the necessity of activity by believing Christians.

[29]*Or is God the God of Jews only? Is he not the God of Gentiles also? Yes, of Gentiles also, [30]since God is one; and he will justify the circumcised on the ground of their faith and the uncircumcised through their faith. [31]Do we then overthrow the law by this faith? By no means! On the contrary, we uphold the law.*

The argument with the Jews in 2:1—3:20 continues to affect these sentences. The object now is to overcome Jewish, and maybe also Jewish Christian, sectarianism in matters of salvation. Is not God also God of the Gentiles? If God is one, which was an article of faith for the Jews, then yet another proof of God's unity is his single act of justification and the unity of faith among Jewish and Gentile Christians.

The basis of the argument is Jewish monotheism. Monotheism was the central idea of the Jewish missionary effort, but in Rom. 3 we can see Paul turning this idea upside down. The Gentiles do not have to be converted to the God of the Jews, but the Jews have to be converted to the God of the Gentiles, to the God who justifies the uncircumcised. This is what Paul regards as the major problem throughout the Epistle to the Romans, not only out of concern for the Jews and their salvation, but above all out of concern for the unity of the church. It is in the church, which Paul describes in 1 Cor. 12 as "the body of Christ," that men encounter in their history the single reality of salvation established by God for both Jews and Gentiles.

Scriptural Proof From Abraham's Righteousness by Faith (4:1–25)

In 3:21 Paul hinted at the testimony of Scripture to the righteousness of God revealed in Christ. He explains this in detail in chapter 4 by means of his proof from Scripture. Paul is not interested merely in the scriptural witness to his argument on justification but also, and chiefly, in the scriptural witness to the conclusion he drew in 3:27–31 from the message of justification, namely, the unity in the church between Jews and Gentiles. For this purpose the figure of Abraham as portrayed in Scripture is ideal. The purpose of the proof from Scripture emerges more clearly as the argument of the chapter develops. First of all we see in what sense we can speak in scriptural terms of Abraham's righteousness by faith.

Abraham's Justification by Faith (4:1–8)

¹*What then shall we say about Abraham, our forefather according to the flesh?* ²*For if Abraham was justified by works,*

he has something to boast about, but not before God. ³For what does the Scripture say? " Abraham believed God, and it was reckoned to him as righteousness." ⁴Now to one who works, his wages are not reckoned as a gift but as his due. ⁵And to one who does not work but trusts him who justifies the ungodly, his faith is reckoned as righteousness. ⁶So David also pronounces a blessing upon the man to whom God reckons righteousness apart from works:

⁷*" Blessed are those whose iniquities are forgiven, and whose sins are covered;*

⁸*blessed is the man against whom the Lord will not reckon his sin."*

The question in the first verse is meant to arouse the attention of the Jews. Abraham is given the honorific title " our fore-father," though the addition " according to the flesh " implies a limitation. The qualification applies to the Jews' relationship to Abraham, and Paul here includes himself with the Jews. Verse 2 makes the connection with the previous chapter clearer: " if Abraham was justified by works . . ." This refers back to the argument of 3:28 and beyond that to the message of 3:21-26. As long ago as Abraham boasting was excluded, excluded by Abraham's faith.

Genesis 15:6 now becomes the main support for the Pauline message of justification. " Abraham believed God . . ." The faith of Abraham is already evidence for the opposition between works of the law and faith—if not explicitly, at least by im-plication. At any rate Paul is able to interpret the quotation from Genesis so that it does not speak of Abraham's merit—which was how Judaism had seen it—but of God's gift of righteousness because of his faith. Faith excludes any pride in one's own merit. For a Jew this is something unheard of. The Jews are convinced by their tradition that Abraham is on their side, their model of piety and confidence in merit, and now Paul snatches away this central figure in the history of salva-tion and makes him a star witness for his message of grace.

Verses 4–5 reveal the real basis of Paul's argument. The "reckoning" of faith, according to him, is not the reckoning of an achievement but a "reckoning by grace," which is awarded to the "one who does not work" but "only" believes. The man who believes is the man who relinquishes all claim to merit reckoned on the basis of his actions. This abandonment of self-assertion is an essential part of faith. In himself man is literally "godless." By recognizing this he allows the justifying action of God to work.

In verses 6–8 Paul supports his interpretation of Gen. 15:6 with another scripture text, Ps. 32:1–2. After Moses (Gen. 15:6) comes David, the prophetically inspired singer of the psalms. The blessing of the psalm, according to Paul, clearly goes to the man to whom God reckons righteousness apart from works. This is of course not the immediate sense of the two verses. They describe the happiness of having one's sins forgiven, and the term "reckon" occurs, which gave Paul the basis for his argument. God does not reckon sin. For Paul this can only be understood in terms of his gospel of grace, as a reckoning not by merit but by grace and therefore apart from works. The argument is complicated, but this is not unusual with Paul.

Abraham the Father of All Who Believe (4:9–17a)

Paul argues from several points of view for the universal application of Abraham's fatherhood, which includes not only the Jews but, according to the evidence of Scripture itself, also, and primarily, those who believe like Abraham. The universal fatherhood of Abraham is therefore based on his faith, which was reckoned to him as righteousness. Paul deals with the scriptural evidence for the universality of Abraham's fatherhood in two stages, first, with reference to the precedence in time and value of faith over circumcision (verses 9–12) and, second, with reference to the precedence in time of faith over the law (verses 13–17a). Not circumcision, but faith, was reckoned as righteousness. The promises were given, not to the law, but to faith.

Abraham's Fatherhood Depends Not on Circumcision But on Faith (4:9–12)

⁹*Is this blessing pronounced only upon the circumcised, or also upon the uncircumcised? We say that faith was reckoned to Abraham as righteousness.* ¹⁰*How then was it reckoned to him? Was it before or after he had been circumcised? It was not after but before he was circumcised?* ¹¹*He received circumcision as a sign or seal of the righteousness which he had by faith while he was still uncircumcised. The purpose was to make him the father of all who believe without being circumcised and who thus have righteousness reckoned to them,* ¹²*and likewise the father of the circumcised who are not merely circumcised but follow the example of the faith which our father Abraham had before he was circumcised.*

Verse 9 gives us the main point of this exposition: does what Scripture says apply to the circumcised, or does it not also apply to the uncircumcised? The question brings us back to the Jew-Gentile problem which caused so much trouble in Paul's church at this time. To prove the universality of salvation by means of the question whether Abraham was circumcised or still uncircumcised when the text quoted applied to him carries little conviction with us as a historical argument. But putting such a question enables Paul to find in Scripture the reality of Christ which he has met in faith and which he feels himself called to spread. Paul's scriptural proof is theological, not historical. That in constructing it he uses the exegetical tools available to the Judaism of his time should not surprise the historically based exegesis of today. It will make it all the more important for us to pay attention to the intention behind his exposition rather than tracing in every detail the twists of his argument.

This basic intention is clearly stated in the two parts of the final sentence of 4:11b–12. Verse 11b refers to the uncircumcised, verse 12 to the circumcised. On the evidence of Scripture, Abraham must be regarded as "the father of all who believe without being circumcised." The emphasis here, of course, is on the "all". The detail that they believe without being circumcised is directed particularly to the Jews. They believe as the uncircumcised Abraham believed. His faith was "reckoned" to him as righteousness. The same happens now to those who believe.

But the Jews too are included in this category, insofar as they believe. This is shown by verse 12. Abraham is "the father of the circumcised"—a role in which the Jews gladly claim him— but not in the sense of those who belong to the race of the circumcised, but rather insofar as they follow in the footsteps of Abraham who believed without being circumcised. Indeed, only to that extent is he "our father," as Paul adds finally. Presumably Paul is thinking here of Jewish Christians who, as born Jews, also prided themselves on their descent from Abraham. But though Paul does not dispute this descent in the purely natural sense, he will allow it no value in the wider perspective of the mediation of salvation. If Abraham counts for anything—not just before men but also before God—it is in virtue of his faith and not of his circumcision. The Jewish claim to precedence in virtue of circumcision, which binds them as a people to Abraham, is rejected. Another indication of this is the order of verses 11b–12, first the uncircumcised, then the circumcised.

It is now clear—unpleasantly clear for the Jews—that the example of Abraham shows uncircumcision to be the only true way, not circumcision in itself, of course, but the way of faith recognized by God in the uncircumcised Abraham. This way has now been revealed in the Christ-event as the universal way of salvation, but it is in the main the Gentiles who have discovered it. It is not that uncircumcision has replaced circumcision, but that the claim which was attached to circumcision has lapsed.

The Promise Depended Not on the Law But on Faith (4:13-17a)

¹³*The promise to Abraham and his descendants, that they should inherit the world, did not come through the law but through the righteousness of faith. *¹⁴If it is the adherents of the law who are to be the heirs, faith is null and the promise is void. *¹⁵For the law brings wrath, but where there is no law there is no transgression. *¹⁶That is why it depends on faith, in order that the promise may rest on grace and be guaranteed to all his descendants—not only to the adherents of the law but also to those who share the faith of Abraham, for he is the father of us all, *¹⁷as it is written, "I have made you the father of many nations".* . . .

Paul takes up his proof again in verse 13. The theme is now " promise." The contents of the promise are described in terms of a text such as Gen. 18:18: " Abraham shall become a great and mighty nation, and all the nations of the world shall bless themselves by him." Similarly, there are frequent references to a countless posterity. Paul interprets this promise to mean that Abraham " and his descendants " shall " inherit the world."

Paul here contrasts the law and the " righteousness of faith," again with reference to Abraham. The fact that the law of Moses came only after Abraham gives a certain plausibility to the contrast, although no Jew would have accepted the conclusion Paul draws. For the Jews the promise was made to Abraham on account of. his merits, and it was this promise which the Jews were to share as Abraham's descendants. Once more Paul is trying to establish Abraham as a symbol of the universal church of Jews and Gentiles, here with reference to the promise made to Abraham and fulfilled in Christ.

Verse 14 shows clearly that his starting point is the present reality of faith. But what does it mean to say that faith is null if " the adherents of the law " are the heirs? Is it a case of " intolerable therefore impossible "? Perhaps, but let us examine the argument more closely. Faith would have already been nullified if the Jews were in reality the heirs, but since faith is the reality the claim of the Jews is shown to be null. Those who believe have already inherited the promise in virtue of their faith. Having established this, Paul can proceed.

Verse 15 is Paul's attempt to sum up the argument of the two preceding verses: the law spans the gap between the promise to Abraham and the fulfillment of the promise in the present by the Christ-event. But this is the time without salvation, the time of sin and the wrath of God; and in an afterthought Paul touches on the period before the law—where there is no law there is no transgression. Verse 16 is the climax of the argument. The correspondence between Abraham's faith and the action of God through grace in the present is briefly established, and then a concluding sentence (as in verses 11b–12) sums up the argument so far: the promise is guaranteed to all his descendants. The universal scope of the salvation established in the present is reaffirmed.

Verses 13–17a as a whole make it clear that Paul is arguing for the unity of Jews and Greeks in the one church which derives its existence from Christ, and that his argument is directed at the position of his Jewish contemporaries, which was to some extent shared by Jewish Christians. It is for the argument with the Jews that he needs Abraham, a central figure in the history of salvation, as the main support for his case. But Abraham is not conclusive historical evidence for the historical continuity of God's saving activity, so much as evidence for the consistency of his saving will, which produces a righteousness through faith now as it did in Abraham. Abraham's testimony is that faith in Christ should lead to a universal church. In the rest of the chapter, verses 17b–25, Paul goes on to show that faith in Christ today is identical with Abraham's faith.

Abraham's Faith Is the Model of Ours (4:17b–25)

[17b]—*in the presence of the God in whom he hoped and believed, who gives life to the dead and calls into existence the things that do not exist. [18]In hope he believed against hope, that he should become the father of many nations; as he had been told, " So shall your descendants be."*

The figure of Abraham now comes into the foreground even more than in the last section, this time as a model of faith. Whereas in verses 1–17a the theological significance of Abraham's faith was considered, Paul now concentrates on its inner structure. By hoping against hope Abraham became a model of Christian faith, indeed, in one respect Abraham's faith can be seen to be Christian faith, since he believed in the God who gives life to the dead. This ultimate correspondence between Abraham's faith and Christian faith is the climax of Paul's " proof from Scripture," the final assurance that he has Scripture on his side.

Verse 17 announces the subject, faith in God who gives life to the dead and calls into existence things that do not exist. The phrase " in the presence of God " makes it clear how the previous statements are to be understood. What was said about Abraham's fatherhood is not an abstract truth, but depends on God. That is how Paul wants Abraham to be judged, in the sight of God. God, we might say, is the hermeneutical principle of Paul's interpretation. This was already true in 3:30, where God was proclaimed as the ultimate basis of the church's unity. Now God is made known as the God both of Abraham and of the church: both, Abraham and the church, believe in the God who gives life to the dead.

[19]*He did not weaken in faith when he considered his own body,*

59

which was as good as dead because he was about a hundred years old, or when he considered the barrenness of Sarah's womb. ²⁰*No distrust made him waver concerning the promise of God, but he grew strong in his faith as he gave glory to God,* ²¹*fully convinced that God was able to do what he promised.* ²²*That is why his faith was " reckoned to him as righteousness."*

Verses 19–20 describe the faith of Abraham with the details of the biblical story but here again, as in verses 3ff., the biblical story is lightly retouched. Paul bases his account on Gen. 17:17, according to which Abraham received from God the promise of a son. " Then Abraham fell on his face and laughed, and said to himself, ' Shall a child be born to a man who is a hundred years old? Shall Sarah, who is ninety years old, bear a child?' " However the laughter of Abraham here, and that of Sarah in Gen. 18:12–15, is to be interpreted, the story is clearly not about Abraham's faith but his doubt. Paul emphasizes the natural deadness of the body as the precondition for God's action, and it matters little to him that the Bible clearly doesn't allow us to talk of absolute sterility in Abraham's case, since according to Gen. 25:1–2 Abraham later had six sons by a woman called Ketura. The best solution is not to accuse Paul of inaccuracy or forgetfulness but to accept that his purpose is not to retell biblical history but to evaluate it from the position he has reached through his present experience of the reality of faith.

What Paul is describing in the story of Abraham is Christian faith. It is Christian faith which is called into being by God out of death, which is able to maintain its trust in God's promise against all doubt, and which is certain that the power of God will fulfill the promise (verse 20). All this allows Paul to give Abraham the benefit of the doubt, since Scripture says, " It was reckoned to him as righteousness." Of course Paul does not put it in that order, but the other way round: " because Abraham was like that, scripture says . . ." (verse 22).

²³But the words, " it was reckoned to him," were written not for his sake alone, ²⁴but for ours also. It will be reckoned to us who believe in him that raised from the dead Jesus our Lord, ²⁵who was put to death for our trespasses and raised for our justification.

Verses 23–24 finally leave no doubt about the real reasons for Paul's interest in the story of Abraham; it is for the sake of those who believe today. The biblical texts apply to them, in the sense that the action of God to which the texts bear witness is at work in them. What in the earlier part of the exposition was concealed under the description " Abraham's faith " is now revealed as Christian faith in God, who raised from the dead Jesus, our Lord. This Christological statement is briefly expanded in verse 25 in the language of a credal formula which ends by bringing before us once more the theme of " our justification," in which God's power to raise the dead achieves its end.

FURTHER EXPLANATION
OF THE PROCESS OF JUSTIFICATION

(5:1—8:39)

There is a break between chapters 4 and 5. The beginning of
5:1 shows that Paul intends to draw conclusions: " *Therefore,*
since we are justified by faith . . ." Here he looks back to the
exposition of the justification process in Part 1; the previous
section ended with the key word " justification " (4:26). Now
Paul intends to bring out further implications of the salvation
he has proclaimed as established. What does it mean to say
that we are " justified "? First of all, that we have peace and
rejoice in the hope of sharing the glory of God (5:1-2). The
section begun here goes to the end of chapter 8. But chapters
5-8 have no systematic structure; they are characterized by a
series of new concepts such as " peace," " grace," " hope,"
" love," " Spirit," " reconciliation," " salvation," " life,"
" sanctification," " glory," " sonship." These concepts did not
appear, or very rarely appeared, in Part 1. Their function is to
reveal justification as a process which involves every aspect of
man, though we are certainly never allowed to forget that this
new existence requires further action on the part of man (see
esp. chapters 6 and 8). It is noticeable that the terms " justification " and " righteousness " go more into the background. The
newly introduced terms have to explain in the context of Part 2
what is involved in the " justification " of men. They should be
seen as illustrations of the message of justification. Justification
therefore remains the subject in these chapters, but it is treated
from a different aspect.

The Scope of Justification (5:1–21)

Peace and Hope as Gifts of God's Love (5:1–11)

THE GIFTS (5:1–5)

¹*Therefore, since we are justified by faith, we have peace with God through our Lord Jesus Christ.* ²*Through him we have obtained access to this grace in which we stand, and we rejoice in our hope of sharing the glory of God.* ³*More than that, we rejoice in our sufferings, knowing that suffering produces endurance,* ⁴*and endurance produces character, and character produces hope,* ⁵*and hope does not disappoint us, because God's love has been poured into our hearts through the Holy Spirit who has been given to us.*

" Therefore, since we are justified." In this whole section 5:1–11 Paul speaks mainly in the first person plural: "we" are those who have been touched by the process of justification which has been proclaimed. Paul is here speaking directly to each man and is trying to explore the new self-awareness of those who believe. The time is the present, the time of faith and, above all, as verses 3–4 show, the time of testing. Now we will see what it means to say, " Jesus Christ, our Lord."

The peace we have obtained through Jesus Christ in our relations with God is the gift of God promised to us in the Christ-event. It should not be confused with rest, in the sense of resting on the laurels Christ has won for us. Chapter 6 in particular makes this clear. " Peace " is the eschatological peace towards which, in historical terms, we constantly reach, but which in essence, through the mediation of Jesus Christ, is already " present." " Peace with God " describes this eschatological relationship which, since we are justified, we can already enjoy in the present. To that extent peace is no longer just a longing on the part of man, but a reality. To that extent too man's hope for peace within history is a real hope and not utopian. Christians today should make this part of their message, and commit themselves to work for peace.

Verse 2a is a reminder of the work of Christ: "through him we have obtained access to this grace in which we stand." Those who are justified are called to a "standing" which entitles them to give thanks to him who called them. The demands of the "standing of grace," which is not explored in detail until chapter 6, are already noticeable in verse 2. "Grace" here means the peaceful relationship of those who are justified.

In the same verse, after the gift of faith comes hope. The justified may "rejoice" in this hope without any danger of vain boasting, for hope is something God makes possible for those who believe in Jesus Christ and depend completely on him. The "glory of God" is thus the proper object of hope, which is the future-directed, eschatological aspiration of the present condition of justification. But its being an object of hope does not mean that sharing in glory is simply something to come; it is already present in germ as a result of Christ's work. That is why this hope can be a boast. This sort of rejoicing is rooted in the action of Jesus Christ. To that extent too the hope in which the Christian rejoices is no idle dream.

Verse 3 mentions another boast, "sufferings." What has Paul in mind here? The sufferings he himself has experienced in his apostolic mission (cf. 2 Cor. 11:23–30), or the "weakness" of which he boasts in 2 Cor. 11:30–33? Probably both. But the word "suffering" here is part of the description of the Christian life. If it is part of Christian life to boast of one's hope to share the glory of God, so it is too to boast of sufferings. These sufferings are not just persecutions for the faith, but all the sufferings in which death casts its shadow over our lives: fear, anxiety for the future, disappointments, sufferings, illnesses, difficult circumstances, all the things life brings in its train—all these now have to be accepted as a gift from God. This means that sufferings for the Christian are not simply something which has been overcome but a gift and a task which he has to accept. As regards bearing sufferings, it is no easier for the Christian than the non-Christian. But the Christian, through his faith, can put his sufferings in a context which is not open to the non-Christian. Paul describes the Christian's attitude to suffering, paradoxically, as "rejoicing." Of course this doesn't mean boasting about the sufferings one experiences and talking about them: what it means is simply accepting sufferings in the light of Jesus Christ. A rejoicing of this sort excludes any empty triumphalism.

God's Love the Source of our Life (5:6–11)

⁶While we were yet helpless, at the right time Christ died for the ungodly. ⁷Why, one will hardly die for a righteous man— though perhaps for a good man one will dare even to die. ⁸But God shows his love for us in that while we were yet sinners Christ died for us. ⁹Since, therefore, we are now justified by his blood, much more shall we be saved by him from the wrath of God. ¹⁰For, if while we were enemies we were reconciled to God by the death of his Son, much more, now that we are reconciled, shall we be saved by his life. ¹¹Not only so, but we also rejoice in God through our Lord Jesus Christ, through whom we have now received our reconciliation.

The conclusive demonstration of God's love for us in the history of salvation was Jesus' sacrifice of his life for us (verses 6, 8). "While we were yet helpless . . . Christ died for the ungodly." Men were helpless in the former age because of their hopeless situation; they were "helpless" and "ungodly" because, in spite of their apparent assurance, they were forced to rely totally on God's action. This negative presupposition is the point from which God's loving initiative starts.

Verse 7 emphasizes the unusual nature of Jesus' sacrifice of his life for us. Human relationships in general tell a different story; it is far from normal for one man to suffer for another. This prepares the way for an appreciation of the statement in verse 8: "while we were yet sinners Christ died for us." Verse 9 brings our mind back to verse 5a. Hope finds fulfillment in the future salvation from the wrath of God. Paul here reminds us once more that our view of the future is grounded in the present reality of justified existence. The formal phrase " by his blood " (used also in 3:25—see also 1 Cor. 11:25: " the new covenant in my blood," and Eph. 1:7; Col. 1:20) locates the process of justification in Jesus' sacrifice of his life. This gives us " much more " assurance in our hope. Once more, in verse 10, Paul comes back to the connection between the death of Jesus and eschatological salvation, this time from the standpoint of reconciliation with God: the death of the Son of God overcomes the " enmity " between man and God. His explanation contrasts the death and life of Jesus as " means " in the process of salvation, though of course the two cannot really be separated—indeed it is in his death that Jesus' life breaks through, that life which is also ours (see also 6:11; Gal. 2:20).

The New Man and the New Humanity (5:12–21)

Paul's aim in this section is to explain the scope of the justification achieved in faith in relation to human history. He does this by means of a contrast between Adam and Christ. In this Adam is the representative of all mankind; and just as all mankind was incorporated in the first Adam, so too the second Adam and his actions have universal significance. In understanding this section it is necessary to bear in mind the underlying intention of the contrast between Adam and Christ. It is not enough simply to see what is said about each; we must also see the connection.

The Link Between Sin and Death (5:12–14)

[12]*Therefore as sin came into the world through one man and death through sin, and so death spread to all men because all men sinned . . .*

66

The previous verses have emphasized the work of Jesus Christ, and this section connects with them, as is indicated by the first word, "therefore." Paul now intends to make a comparison: "just as through one man . . ."—but after this beginning the contrast between the action of Christ and the action of Adam is not continued. We are left with the statement of one side, Adam's, though the other is not simply abandoned; the missing second half of the sentence is simply displaced by the new idea which is introduced in verses 13–14. This means that verse 12 can only be completely understood in the context of the whole section, verses 12–21.

¹³*Sin indeed was in the world before the law was given, but sin is not counted where there is no law. ¹⁴Yet death reigned from Adam to Moses, even over those whose sins were not like the transgression of Adam, who was a type of the one who was to come.*

Instead of completing the sentence begun in verse 12, Paul digresses in verse 13 to deal with the question whether and how there can be talk of sin before the law was given. Sin, obviously, is a transgression of the law, but since Paul has said in verse 12 that sin is *the sin of all men,* the question now arises how there can be talk of sin when the law (of Moses) was not yet given. In Paul's answer it is now made clear that sin is always both the power of non-salvation inevitably affecting mankind and at the same time the individual man's actions against salvation for which he is personally answerable. Sin did indeed come into the world through Adam's sin, but this sin is not "counted" as the act of newly sinful mankind; there is no "charge" as long as the law is not there to act against salvation. The law has the effect of giving prominence to sin as man's sinful act. "Through the law comes knowledge of sin" (3:20): that is to say, through the law the sin in man's actions becomes aware of itself.

It cannot of course be denied that the power of sin also

reigned over mankind "from Adam to Moses," although (verse 13) sin was not yet counted or, in other words, men's sins "were not like the transgression of Adam" (verse 14). Paul cannot conceive of death without sin, but he tries to distinguish. As a result of the power of sin in the world death is also imaginable at a time when the human action which brought sin to power is not (or not yet) "counted." Without underestimating the theological value of this apostolic statement, we may still feel a certain difficulty. One reason for this is that Paul sees sin, death and the law as powers in alliance against salvation which have made human history into a history of the absence of salvation. Not even the Jews, who boasted of their law, are exempt from the effects of this historical situation.

ADAM'S TRESPASS AND GOD'S FREE GIFT INCOMPARABLE 5:15-17)

¹⁵*But the free gift is not like the trespass. For if many died through one man's trespass, much more have the grace of God and the free gift in the grace of that one man Jesus Christ abounded for many.* ¹⁶*And the free gift is not like the effect of that one man's sin. For the judgment following one trespass brought condemnation, but the free gift following many trespasses brings justification.* ¹⁷*If, because of one man's trespass, death reigned through that one man, much more will those who receive the abundance of grace and the free gift of righteousness reign in life through the one man Jesus Christ.*

Paul does not make a simple parallel between Adam and Christ. In his comparison his chief concern is to stress the wide-ranging effect of Christ's act. This, however, is in itself so incomparable, that a parallel between Adam and Christ can only illustrate the contrast between sin and grace and the transcendence of the trespass by the gift of grace. This explains the emphatic "much more" which recurs so frequently in these verses.

Adam's trespass brought mankind inexorably under the power of death. This situation brought about by God's free gift is different and transcends the old: through the new Adam, Jesus Christ, God's grace is given to men in abundance. Grace appears in Christ's act as an undeserved and immeasurable gift given to those who, left to themselves, could look forward to nothing but the sequence of sin and death.

The complete difference of the situation is emphasized in verse 16. The gift of grace is not like the transition to sin and death, which followed Adam's sin. The judgment following *one* trespass led to condemnation. In contrast, the free gift followed *many* trespasses, and leads to " righteousness."

The emphasis on the one and the many affected by one man needs some explanation. The sevenfold repetition of " one " emphasizes that everything hangs on one man. Mankind is seen as a unity; it owes its existence and status to one man. In Jewish thought unity and uniqueness were attributed first of all to God. " God is one," argues Paul in Gal. 3:20, and takes it for granted that the statement is beyond contradiction. Corresponding to the unity of God is the creation of *one* man (in two complementary sexes which together mirror the unity) as his image. This unity is thus normative for the whole of mankind in the plan of creation, though this does not necessarily involve a genealogical unity. This unity in creation remains normative even when through *one* man's sin it is distorted into a unity in the absence of salvation. Man without Christ is creation distorted, and Paul has described his situation in 1:18—3:20. This absence of salvation is exemplified in verse 16 in the " many trespasses." In Christ the unity originally planned by God in the creation is restored as a *situation of salvation,* so that Christ can now be seen as the *new* Adam, in whom the unity of mankind in salvation is newly established. In the experience of faith directed to Christ, man finally realizes that the unity of the human race rests on the saving will of God which is both prior to and transcends the whole history of the absence of salvation.

Summary and Conclusion: the Universal Reign of Grace (5:18–21)

¹⁸Then as one man's trespass led to condemnation for all men, so one man's act of righteousness leads to acquittal and life for all men. ¹⁹For as by one man's disobedience many were made sinners, so by one man's obedience many will be made righteous. ²⁰Law came in to increase the trespass; but where sin increased, grace abounded all the more, ²¹so that, as sin reigned in death, grace also might reign through righteousness to eternal life in Jesus Christ our Lord.

Taken in the context of the whole passage 5:12–17, the antithesis between Adam and Christ shows the universal effect of Christ's saving act, and Paul sums this up once more in verse 18. As *all* men were deprived of salvation through *one* man, so now *all* men acquire salvation through *one* man, Christ. The main theme of this section is *the universality* of *salvation*. At the end Paul begins to explain how, as sin "reigned in death," now grace is to "reign through righteousness to eternal life." We should notice that in this summary verse 19 once more, and this time more clearly than verse 12, connects the loss of salvation and the sins of all men with *Adam's sin*. This passage leaves it open how we are to understand this connection, since it is mentioned only in contrast to Christ's act. The basic principle for understanding both verse 12 and verse 19, however, is that the statements about Adam's sin and the sins of all men cannot be understood in isolation, but have their meaning in the context of the explanation of Christ's redemptive act and the new self-understanding of the believer.

Verse 20a mentions once more the law's role as an obstacle to salvation. It should be understood in the light of 3:20 and 5:13–14. Verse 20b is to be taken as a simple statement of fact: this is how it has proved to be in the Christ-event; it needed the abundance of grace to counteract a sin only "perfected" by the law. How this idea could be misunderstood we can see from 6:1–2.

The conclusion which Paul in verse 21 draws from this statement leads further to the subject of chapter 6: between sin and grace a *change of rulers* has taken place. This is the basis of the new obligations which now bind mankind justified in faith.

II. A New Way of Life (6:1–23)

That a new start has been made in the act of Jesus Christ and mankind wins life through faith in him means new demands on those who have been justified in faith. The " reign " of Christ's grace is no comfortable enjoyment of a salvation which has been earned; it claims the believer for complete and life-long obedience.

The exhortations in this chapter make it particularly clear that the new life of the justified has to hold its own in a permanent confrontation with sin, which constantly tries to reassert its old claims to authority (cf. especially 6:11–14). Paul's urgent warnings against the old slavery to sin are made all the more necessary by the triumphant tones in which he has just proclaimed the basically unassailable reality of the process of justification. The more triumphant the message of grace, the more forceful must be the exhortations to a new way of life and the warnings against sin.

Dead to Sin—alive to God (6:1–14)

¹*What shall we say then? Are we to continue in sin that grace may abound? ²By no means! How can we who died to sin still live in it?*

It was all too easy to make a convenient principle out of Paul's remark in 5:20b: the more we sin, the more grace we get. Paul had already had to reject this misinterpretation of his message in 3:8, and he now attacks it once more in order to bring out the correct conclusions demanded by the message of justification.

The opposition between sin and grace is absolute. The grace given in Christ allows no comparison with sin—indeed, what grace means is that sin has lost its power and has no more claims. Grace leaves those who have thus been freed from sin no other choice than to take up the new possibility of life in grace and make it a reality. Grace reveals itself as grace in the process of being taken up by us. It permits no quietism; that would simply lead to a re-establishment of the old sin. No, grace means a new start for those who have received it. Paul makes this clear with the ethical imperative which runs through the whole chapter.

Paul's questions at the very beginning of the chapter point towards this imperative. In accordance with the message of justification, the *new man* is the gratuitous, unearned, freely given new possibility. This can suffer no diminution, and the freedom of those who have been redeemed from sin can in no way be limited by new commandments. But the new man does not become a reality *automatically,* but through complete and constant reliance on the new possibility bestowed by God.

³*Do you not know that all of us who have been baptized into Christ Jesus were baptized into his death? ⁴We were buried with him therefore by baptism into death, so that as Christ was raised from the dead by the glory of the Father, we too might walk in newness of life. ⁵For if we have been united with him in a death like his, we shall certainly be united with him in a resurrection like his. ⁶We know that our old self was crucified with him so that the sinful body might be destroyed, and we might no longer be enslaved to sin. ⁷For he who has died is freed from sin.*

Paul reminds us of baptism. By baptism we experienced the death of Jesus in our own bodies. We are baptized into his death, and that means "buried with him into death" (verse 4). This passage gives us little indication of how we are to imagine the link with Christ in baptism, but it is less likely that Paul is thinking of a *mystical* death with Christ than of a resemblance to him which is brought about throughout the life of the Christian and of which baptism is the symbolic initiation: a more literal translation of verse 5 would be "united to the image of his death." But in any event this description should not be limited to the single act of baptism; it refers generally to the whole course of the Christian's life. This fits the argument of the chapter as a whole. The "new life" to which the baptized gain access *through the death of Christ* unfolds in history as they respond freely and without reserve to the constant claim of grace.

In this way the Christian life becomes a credible sign of the hope of fulfillment revealed in the death and resurrection of Jesus. Being united "with the image of Christ's resurrection" is no baseless and empty hope precisely because of the continual realization of the "new life" in Christian existence; it is a hope which works itself out in history, in an existence in which the future union with the image of Christ's resurrection is already visible. Baptism is not just an anticipation of the resurrection to which we look forward, as the enthusiasts in Corinth understood it who had themselves baptized on behalf of the dead (1 Cor. 15), but the basis of the new life of the justified as a sharing of Christ's life in hope.

In verse 6 Paul returns to the Christ-event and our being patterned after it. That "our old self" was crucified with him in baptism, the symbolic and effective opening of the *new* reality, has far-reaching consequences. The "sinful body" was to be destroyed, and sin was to find no further purchase on the existence of the baptized. In the mystery of Christ and correspondingly in baptism the break with sin is absolute. Man is now *free* from sin. This freedom, based on Christ and determined by him, now has to prove itself by opposing every claim or assault by sin on the existence of the justified.

73

[8]But if we have died with Christ, we believe that we shall also live with him. [9]For we know that Christ being raised from the dead will never die again; death no longer has dominion over him. [10]The death he died he died to sin, once for all, but the life he lives he lives to God. [11]So you also must consider yourselves dead to sin and alive to God in Christ Jesus.

Once again Paul stresses the *hope* which has been opened up for us in the death of Christ. The death and raising of Jesus are not to be understood only as the unique and unrepeatable saving event of history, the ultimate legitimation of all Christian hope, but they also *represent* our existence before God. Just as Christ died to sin and now lives to God, so we too are dead to sin but alive to God (verse 11). This fact rescues the phenomenon of Christ from the remoteness of a fading past and makes Jesus Christ and his sacrifice of his life the permanent, experienced basis of our existence. Thus the triumphant affirmation in verse 9, " death no longer has dominion over him," should be understood with reference not just to the " private " past and future existence of Jesus but to that of all who are alive " in Christ Jesus."

If there is no further mention of baptism in these verses, that is not because it has been simply forgotten. It is still relevant from its mention in 6: 3-5. Paul's object in mentioning baptism was to emphasize the obligations of the new life as a way of existence permanently influenced by Christ. But we should notice that in the whole context the mention of baptism has only supplementary value; in chapter 6 too the previously proclaimed message of justification is the mainstay of Paul's argument. We will therefore misinterpret him if we connect all the individual statements in this paragraph directly and exclusively with baptism. All the subsidiary statements are meant to contribute to explaining the basis of the Christian life.

[12]Let not sin therefore reign in your mortal bodies, to make you obey their passions. [13]Do not yield your members to sin as

instruments of wickedness, but yield yourselves to God as men who have been brought from death to life, and your members to God as instruments of righteousness. [14]*For sin will have no dominion over you, since you are not under law but under grace.*

The consequences mentioned in the previous passage are now further discussed. *Sin will have no dominion.* The imperative of moral demands now comes into the foreground, though in the form of a warning. Christians have to be constantly warned against the dominion of sin. Sin, in principle, deprived of power by Christ, nevertheless remains a negative possibility for Christians. Unless he takes hold of the only true possibility, that offered by grace, he will fall, in spite of the redemptive work of Christ, into the old power of sin. But Christians cannot allow themselves such " comfort." Old sin's foothold is " our mortal body " with its " passions." It is the " old self " and its " body " on which sin always builds (verse 6). If the Christian constantly opposes sin and relies on his relationship with Christ, the " destruction " of the " body of sin " (verse 6) is continually accomplished: sin is deprived of its remaining hold on the existence of the Christian and a new " embodiment " of sin is prevented. Perhaps it is hardly necessary to mention that Paul should not be accused of hostility to the body because of these verses; he calls for " full-bodied " obedience to God (verse 13).

But before Paul shows the positive side of this ethical imperative, he once more stresses his point that Christian life is a rejection of sin (verse 13). The lives of Christians are an offering of themselves to God, to whom they owe their rescue from death and call to life. This offering of self to God is carried out in the gift of their " members " as " instruments of righteousness " and not of wickedness.

Verse 6:14 refers back to 5:21: between sin and grace a " change of rulers " has taken place. The new rule of grace claims man completely and tolerates no compromise with sin.

75

15What then? Are we to sin because we are not under the law but under grace? By no means! 16Do you not know that if you yield yourselves to any one as obedient slaves, you are slaves of the one whom you obey, either of sin, which leads to death, or of obedience, which leads to righteousness?

Verse 15 repeats the question of verse 1, and begins a new, more urgent exposition of the moral requirements of the justified. The key words are now " slaves of sin," " slaves of righteousness," " obedience " and " freedom."

The believer is under grace—there is no doubt about that. But he must now take hold in faith of the *new reality* which has been given him and make it *his possibility*. This is done in the gift of oneself " as an obedient slave." The question in verse 16 does not just refer to a familiar rule but is concerned wholly with the believer's life of complete obedience. The idea of *being a slave* emphasizes the connection the Christian makes with this offering of himself. Paul uses comparisons from his environment, in this case from the generally accepted rules of his society. Their application goes as far as Paul indicates in the context. His use of the image of slavery to apply to Christianity results first from the contrast with " slavery to sin." This is the counterpart to slavery in the strict sense, while Christians are " set free for freedom " (Gal. 5:1; cf. Gal. 5:13). This means that the description of the Christian's " enslavement " to God or to righteousness (verse 18) is to be understood first of all as a contrast, though it does emphasize the relationship to Christ which is based on the believer's obedience and which preserves him from slavery to sin.

17But thanks be to God, that you who were once slaves of sin have become obedient from the heart to the standard of teaching to which you were committed, 18and, having been set free from sin, have become slaves of righteousness.

In the light of Christ the relationships are clear and unmistakable, and this prompts Paul to give thanks to God. Since Christ slavery to sin is the form of the past. The present is characterized by the obedience of believers, for which Christ has set them free. Verse 17b is a parenthesis which it is difficult to relate to the context. It refers to the binding force of "teaching," which presents the content of Christian faith in a definite form.

20When you were slaves of sin, you were free in regard to righteousness. 21But then what return did you get from the things of which you are now ashamed? The end of those things is death. 22But now that you have been set free from sin and have become slaves of God, the return you get is sanctification and its end, eternal life. 23For the wages of sin is death, but the free gift of God is eternal life in Christ Jesus our Lord.

In verses 20–21 Paul once more reminds his readers of the *sinful past,* in exhortation and warning. As "slaves of sin" they had an appearance of freedom, inasmuch as they were unaware of the power of God's righteousness which brings about salvation and makes demands on man. But looking back, the justified are "ashamed" of the "return" brought by slavery to sin, a "return" which finally reveals itself as death.

"But now" (cf. 3:21), in the present, marked by the liberating act of Jesus and the new obedience of the justified, we can talk of a genuine "return." It is the "return" from the "self-offering" of the justified which is seen in "sanctification" —not simply as a defensive separation from the sinful world, but as a demonstration of the sanctifying power of grace in constant opposition to the ever-present threat of sin. Its final and decisive manifestation is the long-awaited fulfillment of "eternal life." Verse 23 concludes the contrast between the wages of the old service of sin and the new service of God.

It is impossible not to notice how, in spite of the positively worded call to a new way of life, the dominant note of the chapter is the exhortation not to fall back into sin. This finds its more positive complement in Rom. 12–13. The apostle's appeal to his readers there makes clear that, while Christian character must remain conscious of the threat of sin, it shows itself also, and above all, in the practice of the love which changes the world.

Between Law and Freedom (7:1–25)

The new obedience to which we have been called, our new possibility based on the life given to us by Christ, leads to crisis. The new life means a constant rejection by the believer of his own sinful past. This past was essentially overcome in Christ, but it makes itself felt again in anyone who does not make full use of Christ's liberating act as liberation from the law. The law awakens sin, and is thus an instrument of death not life. The Christian has to realize quite clearly that Christian freedom and the life of obedience it implies is not easy.

This is why Paul in verses 1–6 once more takes as his subject the freedom of the Christian as freedom from the law. The two paragraphs which follow, verses 7–12 and 13–25, discuss the question of the law. They examine first of all the ambiguity of the law as God's good demand and as a factor opposing salvation in association with sin and death. In a digression he explains more precisely the scope of the freedom from the law which he has proclaimed. His explanation, however, is more important than a mere digression, because it is the law's activity in co-operation with sin against salvation which makes the Christian aware of the desperate situation from which he has been freed; it shows him how much he needs to be on his guard against losing the new freedom and slipping back into the old state, dominated by the law and sin.

Legal Proof of Freedom from the Law (7:1–6)

¹Do you know, brethren—for I am speaking to those who know the law—that the law is binding on a person only during his life? ²*Thus a married woman is bound by the law to her husband as long as he lives; but if her husband dies she is discharged from the law concerning the husband.* ³*Accordingly, she will be called an adulteress if she lives with another man while her husband is alive. But if her husband dies she is free from that law, and if she marries another man she is not an adulteress. Likewise, my brethren, you have died to the law through the body of Christ, so that you belong to another, to him who has been raised from the dead in order that we may bear fruit for God.*

Because the Christian has to realize that thanks to Christ he is now a free man and owes no more tribute to the powers of the former age his very freedom faces him with a problem in that it breaks every tie with his own past. This must have been a particular difficulty for Jewish Christians, for whom, because of their Jewish tradition, the Mosaic law could not be a matter of unimportance. It is for these Jewish Christians that Paul has to prove the scope of his message of freedom from the law. It is true that his argument proves that the release from the law is valid under the terms of the law not just for Jews or Jewish Christians, but for all Christians, who to a greater or lesser degree are affected by the inheritance of the Jewish law, constantly working to cast doubt on and limit the freedom they have acquired and the confidence Christ has won for them. Freedom must be taken seriously as freedom from the law. This is the point behind Paul's not altogether watertight proof from analogy with marriage law.

Paul starts from a generally recognized principle, that the law's claim on a person lapses with his death—perhaps in view of 6:3ff., dying with Christ is at the back of his mind. He tries to illustrate this in verses 2–3 with reference to Christian freedom by a comparison with the law concerning marriage. When her first husband dies, a wife is free and can belong to another— as verse 3 puts it, when the husband dies, she is free from the law. That is Paul's real point, freedom from the law. It makes little difference to him that in verse 1 freedom is given by the person's death whereas in verse 3 the dead first husband represents the law. The real point breaks through the image.

Verse 4 gives us the conclusion in a rather surprising form. Christians have died through the body of Christ—this corresponds to the premise in the first verse. But combined with it is the conclusion from verse 3—you now belong to another. The fact that in verse 3 it was not the woman who lived with another man who died or was killed but the first husband, who stood for the law, is now overlooked and is regarded by Paul as unimportant in comparison with the real conclusion. What looked like a legalistic proof now turns out to be a piece of theological rhetoric.

⁵While we were living in the flesh, our sinful passions, aroused by the law, were at work in our members to bear fruit for death. ⁶But now we are discharged from the law, dead to that which held us captive, so that we serve not under the old written code but in the new life of the Spirit.

Belonging to Christ proves itself in life as fruitful. Verse 5 contrasts this new fruitfulness with the old, the same contrast as at the end of chapter 6. The time of " bearing fruit to death " is essentially past, just as " existence in the flesh " is past. "Flesh" here does not mean simply human nature, but man's existence dominated by sin and thrown back on its own helplessness before and without Christ. If a man is nothing more than "flesh," he is in a bad way, but if the life of faith is active in his " flesh " (cf. Gal. 2:20), the hopelessness of man's earthly existence is decisively broken.

" But now (cf. 3:21; 6:22) we are discharged from the law . . . so that we serve in the newness of the Spirit (or " in the new Spirit ") and no longer in the old way of the written law-code " (verse 6). " New " and " old " describe the contrast between the present of salvation and the past without hope of salvation. The past was dominated by the Mosaic law written on stone (cf. 2 Cor. 3:3–6). The present is under the power of the Spirit, who constantly makes things " new." But the Christian must be always aware that " new " can become " old " if the " new " does not take root in his " service " as the eschatological quality of his existence created by the Spirit.

The Law Is the Past, No Longer the Present (7:7–25)

THE LAW IS NEVERTHELESS GOOD (7:7–12)

⁷What then shall we say? That the law is sin? By no means! Yet, if it had not been for the law, I should not have known sin. I should not have known what it is to covet if the law had not said, " You shall not covet." ⁸But sin, finding opportunity in the commandment, wrought in me all kinds of covetousness. Apart from the law, sin lies dead. ⁹I was once alive apart from the law, but when the commandment came, sin revived and I died; ¹⁰the very commandment which promised life proved to be death to me. ¹¹For sin, finding opportunity in the commandment, deceived me and by it killed me. ¹²So the law is holy, and the commandment is holy and just and good.

The question from which Paul starts seems rather theoretical to us. It has nevertheless a practical basis. " Is the law sin? " is a question which could be prompted by the proof of Christian freedom from the law and the message of justification as a whole. Paul leaves no doubt that the law does not bring salvation, but has proved itself to be simply an ally of sin; it stands among the enemies of salvation. But a Jew in particular could never accept this assertion; the law is and remains the law of God mediated through Moses. It is from this point of view that Paul rejects the conclusion implied in the question. He now tries to make further distinctions: " if it had not been for the law, I should not have known sin." This takes us back to 3:20: "through the law comes knowledge of sin." Since Paul uses the first person singular, we may ask whether he is speaking from his own experience or thinking of men generally. Perhaps the two are not exclusive, and in any case we shall have to look more closely at this " I " in what follows.

Paul's example of the experience of sin concerns the commandment, "You shall not covet." These are the words of the ninth commandment of the Decalogue (Ex. 20:17; Dt. 5:21), but in this passage Paul has in mind the fall of the first man, as is shown by the continuation in verse 8. Adam's fall is a clear illustration of how sin "finds an opportunity in the commandment," and awakens all kinds of covetousness "in me." This corresponds to Paul's assertion that without the law sin is " dead," that is, ineffectual. When the law in this way acts as an enemy of salvation it belongs to the past.

Verses 9–11 add detail to the experience of the " I " with the law. In an "autobiographical" description the " I " relives its past. The paradise story is still in the background, and in accordance with this we can distinguish a time before the law or commandment and a time of the law. The tenor of the whole description gives no basis for a psychological interpretation of the experience of sin under the influence of the law, but simply once more emphasizes the contrast between the law, which is good in itself, and its role as an enemy of salvation. The law is at the same time "holy and just and good" (verse 12) and " death " (verse 10).

It is legitimate to ask once more at this point how seriously Paul intends this " apologia " for the law. Is it merely a concession to the Jews or the Jewish Christians, or does he really allow that the law may have positive value? The question can only be answered by a consideration of Paul's preaching as a whole, and the first point which emerges from that is that since Christ the law can have no positive saving function. Adherence to the law as a means of salvation would go against the grace which is Christ's gift. Jesus' action supersedes the law as God's command. It is for the benefit of those Jewish

Christians who though under grace still want to hope in the law that Paul gives this reminder that the law produced not salvation, but its absence.

The Law Proved Powerless, But Sin Powerful (7:13-25)

[13]Did that which is good, then, bring death to me? By no means! It was sin, working death in me through what is good, in order that sin might be shown to be sin, and through the commandment might become sinful beyond measure.

Sin, death, and law are connected. These three reveal themselves in the former age as powers in alliance. This is why Paul has such difficulty in keeping a special place for the law in this unholy alliance. It is not the law as such, he argues, but sin, which only comes into its own through the law, which is the death-dealing power. The law reveals itself as powerless because it does not bring the life which comes through Christ alone. If we still wish to speak of a " positive " function of the law, it can only be its unmasking of sin in its full sinfulness, which reveals the lack of salvation of man without Christ.

[14]We know that the law is spiritual; but I am carnal, sold under sin.

This sentence makes Paul's argument even more involved. His apologia for the law is still in his mind, and this is why he can call the law " spiritual," while in 2 Cor. 3:3ff. the letter of the law is contrasted with the Spirit and the spiritual dispensation of the New Covenant. It is spiritual because it is God's law. But we need to amplify the meaning: it was not able to impart its spiritual nature to those who were under the law; it did not prove to be a life-giving law. On the contrary, men bound under the law showed themselves to be carnal, because sin found scope in them—not least through the law.

[15]I do not understand my own actions. For I do not do what I want, but I do the very thing I hate. [16]Now if I do what I do not want, I agree that the law is good.

These verses describe the powerlessness of the " I " in sin's grip. The " I " can no longer recognize itself in its own actions. Where does the sin I find in my actions come from if I do not will it. If I sin against my will this discrepancy between action and will shows my utter helplessness and, as regards the law, shows that it " is good "—in contrast to me. My will participates in the law's goodness by accepting the law and because man's will has been directed by his creator towards the good. But in man's activity this direction towards good intended by the creator is constantly distorted into its opposite. We can now see that man under the power of sin does not suffer from a psychological split between action and will, which could perhaps be remedied by psychiatric means, but from a more deeply rooted collapse within his creaturely existence. Even when he does evil and gives himself over in his whole existence to sin, he cannot deny his tie as a creature with God. Man given up to sin cannot get past God.

[17]So then it is no longer I that do it, but sin which dwells within me. [18]For I know that nothing good dwells within me, that is, in my flesh. I can will what is right, but I cannot do it. [19]For I do not do the good I want, but the evil I do not want is what I do. [20]Now if I do what I do not want, it is no longer I that do it, but sin which dwells within me.

The first impression one gets from verse 17 is that the " I " is trying to escape responsibility for the failure of its actions : " it is no longer I that do it, but sin which dwells within me." But this passage is not concerned with a man's subjective responsibility for his individual sin, which Paul in this context has no wish to deny. The statement that " sin which dwells within me " acts does not cancel out the " I do " of verse 15. The important phrase is " no longer." In its actions the " I " is no longer " I ";

the " I " which no longer behaves as " I " is only a dwelling in which sin "dwells." Sin has expropriated the " I," with the result that it has become " not-I."

Verse 18 develops the statement of the non-identity of the " I " under the power of sin, but from a negative aspect. We are told that " nothing good dwells within me." Good is the opposite of sin; it is what ought to be, in this context, what belongs to the identity of the " I." The " I " is once again imagined in a mythological way as an inhabitable space. In an explanatory addition Paul calls the " I " " my flesh." This addition brings out the real weakness of the " I," which allows the " I " to be constantly turned into a " not-I " under the pressure of sin. Verse 19 repeats the message of verse 15, and verse 20 finally takes us back to verse 17.

[21]*So I find it to be a law that when I want to do right, evil lies close at hand.* [22]*For I delight in the law of God, in my inmost self,* [23]*but I see in my members another law at war with the law of my mind and making me captive to the law of sin which dwells in my members.* [24]*Wretched man that I am! Who will deliver me from this body of death?*

These verses conclude the autobiography of the " I " and its sinful past. Verse 21 introduces a conclusion: " so I find it to be a law." Paul uses " law " here to describe the helplessness of the " I " in the power of sin. In this section he uses the idea of " law " not simply in the sense of the Mosaic law or the law of God, but punningly, in a " metaphorical " sense, to describe the irrevocably split state of man under " the law of sin and death " (8:2).

It is important to notice that a positive characteristic of the " I " is mentioned in these verses, and not just its non-identity; it would be wrong to take the description of the " I " as " not-I " as an absolute negation. In verse 18b we find " I can will what is right but I cannot do it," and similarly verse 15 presupposes a will to do good. In verse 16 the " I " is said to accept the law, and verse 22 says the same: " I delight in the law of God, in my inmost self." The main point of all these statements is, of course, an inability to do good.

It is easy to get the impression from this combination of positive and negative statements of a basically divided existence of the " I." We have already drawn attention to verse 15 to avoid giving the impression that our terminology is intended to be psychological. The divided state of human behavior which Paul describes—the fact that action and will are not in accord—is meant to illustrate the " alienation " of the " I " under the power of sin. The " I " still exists, insofar as it wants to do good, but it is at the same time set over against itself because sin has taken possession of it. It is in a real sense " possessed." Paul's language is intended, not as a description of man as a being permanently divided within himself, but to convey the malevolent power of sin in man. Sin is helped into power, surprising though it may seem, not simply by the law but also by the acceptance of the law by the " I." Just as Paul can say in verses 7–11 that the sin did not come without the law, it is equally true that there is no sin without the " I." In this way the " I " allies itself with the forces of the former age, and as a result of their contradictory alliance becomes the " incarnation " in history of sin, which is the commander of these forces. The result is that the " I," though directed towards good, becomes " not-I " under the power of sin, a hopeless and abandoned existence whose hopelessness finally wins utterance in the cry of misery in verse 24.

[25]*Thanks be to God through Jesus Christ our Lord! So then, I of myself serve the law of God with my mind, but with my flesh I serve the law of sin.*

This verse gives the answer to the cry for help in verse 24. " Thanks be to God " is not, of course, a direct answer, but is there really any answer to the hopelessly ruined existence of man in sin? At least there is no answer in the sense of information about how man could free himself. The Christian in particular must bear in mind the unhappy situation of man abandoned in sin. His own "Thanks be to God" cannot mean that he knows he is saved and so can forget about his sinful past. It is for the benefit of Christians that Paul has portrayed the situation of man abandoned in sin in chapter 7, as a description of their own background, from which they have only escaped by God's grace. Christians have to take seriously the old slavery to sin as their "negative possibility," or perhaps better their "lack of possibility."

Verse 25b does not really go with the preceding expression of thanksgiving. It is a final attempt to sum up the divided state of man under sin in a formula. It is probably a later addition by a reader or copyist trying to sum up the difficult argument of the chapter.

The Freedom of the Sons of God as Present and Future (8:1–39)

Chapter 7 has given us the reason for Paul's continual insistence on exhorting his converts to a new way of life. The sinful past of man "in Christ" has indeed been basically overcome, and man "in Christ" is really a "new creation"; he has passed over from death to life. But the Christian is never so far removed from his sinful past that it cannot rise up before him once more in the present as his negative possibility. The Christian is in need of exhortation to a new way of life for this reason; the new life does not produce its effect automatically, but only insofar as man responds to its appeal.

Chapter 8 stresses that the exhortation can only be properly understood in the context of his message of freedom. He first of all recalls the liberating act of Christ in order to appeal to the freedom of those who have been liberated and now walk in the Spirit. They are "sons of God" and "heirs" of his future "glory," and as such they must make good use of the gifts of freedom in the present.

Freedom Through the Spirit (8 : 1–11)

> [1]*There is therefore now no condemnation for those who are in Christ Jesus.* [2]*For the law of the Spirit of life in Christ Jesus has set me free from the law of sin and death.* [3]*For God has done what the law, weakened by the flesh, could not do: sending his own Son in the likeness of sinful flesh and for sin, he condemned sin in the flesh,* [4]*in order that the just requirement of the law might be fulfilled in us, who walk not according to the flesh but according to the Spirit.*

The contrast between verse 1 and the cry of the unredeemed man in 7 : 24 is absolute. " Now "—the glance turns from the unhappy man caught under sin and the law away to the present. In the present which is determined by Christ there is no longer any condemnation for those who are in Christ Jesus. In Christ the old dominion of the powers hostile to salvation has been broken and the new life, the true life, has begun. As a result those who are " in Christ " no longer face the charge of sin. This attitude runs through the whole chapter. This is the Christian's assurance of salvation, which he only possesses in Christ and can only keep by life according to his Spirit.

Liberation from " the law of sin and death " is said in 8 : 2 to be the work of a " law " opposed to the old law. It is the law which is given through the " Spirit," not through the human spirit but through the Spirit whose effect is felt as " life in Christ Jesus." It is finally none other than the Spirit of Jesus Christ himself, who communicates himself to believers and becomes a " new law " for them. But Paul is not proclaiming some sort of new Christian law in place of the old Mosaic law. What is new in his proclamation is the gospel, and that can certainly not be called a law in the strict sense, or a substitute for another law. Paul has here constructed an antithesis, and it is only within the limits of the antithesis that the gospel can be described as " the law " which promulgates freedom.

The process of liberation cannot be imagined without the

work of Jesus Christ and, within that, God's initiative. What the law could not do—instead of life, it led to sin and death—God achieved through his Son. He sent his Son (cf. Gal. 4:4) in the "likeness" of our fleshly mode of existence, dominated by sin. We can feel in the way Paul formulates this idea his effort, on the one hand to describe the Son of God as having become man and taken on himself all the historical conditions of human existence (here summed up in the idea of the "flesh" dominated by sin), and on the other hand not to make the humanity of God's son appear personally sinful. The main weight of the statement, however, lies on the place in salvation history of the Son of God made man. It was on account of mankind fallen into sin that he came, to meet sin in its own sphere of activity, "in the flesh." Paul has in mind the saving event of Christ's death on the cross. In Christ's offering of his life for us, that is, in our place and for our benefit, the sending of God's son achieved its end. In his death Jesus suffered God's judgment on sin and by so doing represented all mankind under sin.

Verse 8:4 passes on to life "according to the Spirit." What Jesus did once for all, he did for us. The transition which his liberating act involves must now find its echo in our new way of life in a transition from flesh to Spirit, and this must be a permanent process. In a life according to the Spirit the just requirement of the law is fulfilled, in virtue of that fulfillment made once for all by the liberating act of Jesus Christ. In fact, the man guided by the Spirit of Christ no longer experiences the just requirement of God as "law"—in its strict sense this term is reserved for the old law of non-salvation—but as the demand of the Spirit himself, who not only requires the new way of life but above all makes it possible.

⁵For those who live according to the flesh set their minds on the things of the flesh, but those who live according to the Spirit set their minds on the things of the Spirit. ⁶To set the mind on the flesh is death, but to set the mind on the Spirit is life and peace. ⁷For the mind that is set on the flesh is hostile to God; it does not submit to God's law, indeed, it cannot; ⁸and those who are in the flesh cannot please God.

Man's possibilities depend on his being. What is man? In himself simply " flesh "! Chapter 7 established this at length. " Flesh " is the superficial earthly existence of man in contrast to his vocation to win life. Now, in the time of faith, we find that life is only granted through the Spirit of Christ. A man has to let himself be led by this Spirit, and only to the degree that he responds to the gift and the demand of this Spirit does he live " according to the Spirit."

We must remember that Paul sees man as completely determined by Christ and his saving work, and therefore we should not expect from him reflections on " man in himself." Paul certainly talks about " man for himself," the man who is worried and concerned for himself and who sins by not really letting God care for him because basically he hopes for salvation not from God but from himself, and can only trust himself to look after his own good and find life. But in reality this man finds only death, and his existence reveals itself from God's point of view as hostility to God. Paul leaves us in no doubt that the only possibility for the Christian of fulfilling God's will is a life guided by the Spirit of Christ.

⁹But you are not in the flesh, you are in the Spirit, if the Spirit of God really dwells in you. Anyone who does not have the Spirit of Christ does not belong to him. ¹⁰But if Christ is in you, although your bodies are dead because of sin, your spirits are alive because of righteousness. ¹¹If the Spirit of him who raised Jesus from the dead dwells in you, he who raised Jesus from the dead will give life to your mortal bodies also through his Spirit who dwells in you.

Paul addresses Christians directly as those who are " in the Spirit." The fundamental reality of this new being is " the

Spirit of God *in you*." " Spirit of God " and " Spirit of Christ " are one and the same. The crucial factor is that the " Spirit " is experienced as the reality which determines the present, both in the lives of individual believers and in the totality and communion of believers, in the community. It is surely no accident that Paul here addresses man " in Christ " in the plural, in contrast to man before and without Christ in chapter 7. The Spirit given to the believer is always the Spirit imparted to the Church of Jesus Christ, though of course the guiding power of the Spirit is also felt in the communion of believers as the new life of each individual.

" In the Spirit " we experience the life produced by the Spirit. But as life involves the whole man, so the Spirit has an effect on the whole man. This is what is meant by the dialectical formulation which speaks of the " body " which is " dead because of sin " and the " Spirit " which is " alive because of righteousness " (verse 10). Both " body " and " spirit " describe the whole man, each from a different point of view. " Spirit " here means the new basis of life, which so totally takes hold of a man that he is now " dead " to sin.

The Spirit bestows life, which means the life of the resurrection. The life the believer lives in the present is the life of Christ who has been raised from the dead and a participation in advance in the future raising of " our mortal bodies," which also takes place because of the Spirit who lives in us. Our present possession of the Spirit should never lead us to mistake the real gift of the Spirit, the inaccessible life of the future which God has promised us.

Life in the Spirit (8 : 12–17)

¹²*So then, brethren, we are debtors, not to the flesh, to live according to the flesh—*¹³*for if you live according to the flesh you will die, but if by the Spirit you put to death the deeds of the body you will live.* ¹⁴*For all who are led by the Spirit of God are sons of God.* ¹⁵*For you did not receive the spirit of*

slavery to fall back into fear, but you have received the spirit of
sonship. When we cry "Abba, Father!" [16]*it is the Spirit him-*
self bearing witness with our spirit that we are children of
God, [17]*and if children, then heirs, heirs of God and fellow-heirs*
with Christ, provided we suffer with him in order that we may
also be glorified with him.

Being " in the Spirit " and now living by the standard of the
Spirit, we are free because of the liberating action of God. In
this freedom we are " debtors " to God, but not of course to
the " flesh." The life of the man who relies on his " flesh," that
is, on himself, inevitably leads to death; quite different is the
fate of us who " by the Spirit put to death the deeds of the
body," that is to say, the sinful activity to which the " body,"
man's " I," was constantly inclined. This activity must be " put
to death " by the Spirit, who leads us to a new Christian
activity, for which he also gives us the power.

Being now free, we are really " sons of God " (verse 14); the
Spirit we have received is not the " spirit of slavery " but the
" spirit of sonship," which gives us a new relationship to God
as his children (8 : 15). The new position of the newly freed as
" sons of God," in virtue of God's saving action enjoying the
full rights of " children of God " (8 : 16; cf. Gal. 4 : 4–7) corresponds to the liberating act of the " Son of God " (verses 2–4).
Paul recalls the new relationship to God which Christians have
obtained in order to stress once again God's gift of freedom as
the basis of the new Christian way of life.

Just as the Christians' sonship has its origin in the action of
the Son of God, so Christians in their lives correspond to him,
in " suffering with him " in the present and " being glorified
with him " in the future. It is significant that Paul describes
the present situation of salvation more precisely as shared suffering attached to the promise of future glory. The children of God
experience their glorification for the present in their new way of
life as a " not yet " in a context of " present achievement." This,

however, does not mean disappointment but promise and hope. It is just this secure knowledge of God's promise in the experience of the Spirit which not only enables us to sustain the struggles of the present but also gives us hope for the future. Life in the Spirit does not therefore make us leap enthusiastically over existence in this transitory world but gives it a new meaning for us.

A Sure Hope (8 : 18–30)

18I consider that the sufferings of this present time are not worth comparing with the glory that is to be revealed to us.

The apostle's appeal to believers to be aware of their new dignity as " sons of God " ended in verse 17 with the promise that those who now " suffer with " Christ would in the future be " glorified with " him. This introduces the subject which dominates the next verse, the Christian's hope for the future. This is of central importance. It is no accident that the second main section of the epistle ends in the promise of the future guaranteed by God for those who are justified by faith.

Christian hope for the future has its basis in God and his liberating activity in the death and resurrection of Jesus. Talk of " future glory " must have this basis in Christ. When the Christian then looks beyond the new life which has begun in him towards the future and tries to reach this future, this " straining forward to what lies ahead " (Phil. 3 : 13) is not selfish impatience but the Christian's duty in the present. The new life which Christians have already received calls of itself for its fulfillment in " glory." The faith by which we are justified bears in itself the promise of future glory. This means that the Christian lives by faith in such a way that he allows the promise for the future to come to fulfillment. A faith which only looked backwards and was limited to the single completed event of redemption in Christ, and was as a result overconfident, would have lost an essential part of its Christian character, the vision of future glory which is also a spur to Christian activity in the present.

The present is marked by " sufferings," the sufferings of the end-time, the sufferings which arise for the Christian from the age which is passing away, out of its inadequacies, mistakes and disappointments, which constantly prevent the " new creation " which has dawned in Christ from shining in its full splendor. These include not only the more or less private sufferings and sorrows of the individual believer but also the social distress of the whole of mankind, which, in various forms in the course of history, summons believers to counter it with aid which also contains within it the seeds of the future. This perspective of future glory cannot in any circumstances leave believers inactive in the face of present sufferings, but should make them bear witness to the " new creation," mindful of the " revolutionary " energy of hope, in Christian praxis.

[19]*For the creation waits with eager longing for the revealing of the sons of God;* [20]*for the creation was subjected to futility, not of its own will but by the will of him who subjected it in hope; because the creation itself will be set free from its bondage to decay and obtain the glorious liberty of the children of God.*

God's salvation affects the whole of creation. This is why Paul can describe the present situation of creation as an " eager longing." Creation as a whole also exists in virtue of the promise; it is to be incorporated in the " revealing of the sons of God," in their glorification, and in this way to be freed from its own " futility " and attain the " glorious liberty of the children of God." The future glory is clearly seen as belonging in the first place to the " children of God," but Paul always insists that the whole of creation is also to be glorified with them. God's call to men does not isolate them from the rest of creation, indeed it calls them to a " new creation " (2 Cor. 5:17; Gal. 6:15; cf. Is.

65 : 17 : " For behold, I create new heavens and a new earth "). Paul's hopeful view of the future lacks nothing in universality and breadth.

This grand vision of the whole saved creation does not, however, leave Christians unmoved in the present. If creation is waiting for the " revealing of the sons of God," then those who can now call themselves " sons of God," because they are, have to take their responsibility for creation with a quite new seriousness. It is certainly not Christian to leave creation to its certain decline and remain inactive. The " passing away " of creation is part of the process of salvation, a passing into a form more deeply marked by salvation, a form which comes from God. This world which is passing into its salvation therefore has a certain future, and it is the duty of Christians to proclaim it clearly and in all its implications.

[22]We know that the whole creation has been groaning in travail together until now; [23]and not only the creation, but we ourselves, who have the first fruits of the Spirit, groan inwardly as we wait for adoption as sons, the redemption of our bodies. [24]For in this hope we are saved. Now hope that is seen is not hope. For who hopes for what he sees? [25]But if we hope for what we do not see, we wait for it with patience.

Verse 22 stresses again the unity of the whole creation " with us." It is a solidarity in the pain of transitoriness, but the pain includes hope, because in the world that is passing away the " new creation " is being formed.

It is not just the creation as a whole, but also " we ourselves " who " groan." This is all the more remarkable since we have received the " Spirit " as the " first fruits " of future glory. Possession of the Spirit does not eliminate this solidarity in distress with the whole creation. In this distress of transition and proving the strength of the Spirit in the passing world " sonship " suddenly appears more of a blessing for the future, even though we have already acquired the rights of " sons of God " (verses

95

15-17). We wait for it as a blessing of salvation in the future insofar as it means the "redemption of our bodies" from the transitoriness of this passing creation. In this context the present for the Christian is very different from a triumphal existence; it is much more an existence in which man endures distress imposed by the Spirit himself and felt in the form of a permanent tension between the old creation and the new.

The phrase "in this hope we were saved" may sound at first hearing like a restriction, "only in hope." Paul, however, has no such restriction in mind when he speaks of our being saved. He proclaims our redemption, which we have achieved in Christ and which has been sealed by the gift of the Spirit, as a redemption achieved without any doubt. It is a salvation "in hope" in the sense that this proclamation reveals the promise included in our redemption that what is already a reality, but as a foretaste and in a hidden form, will in the future be revealed. The future redemption for which we wait in patience is not a different or a second redemption alongside that achieved in Jesus Christ, but the becoming visible of "what we do not see" (verse 25). The patience Christians require consists precisely in not looking for anything else or another promise which might become visible sooner or more easily and divert our sights from the coming of the true promise. Christian hope is in this way the forerunner of the Lord coming in his glory.

26Likewise the Spirit helps us in our weakness; for we do not know how to pray as we ought, but the Spirit himself intercedes for us with sighs too deep for words. 27And he who searches the hearts of men knows what is in the mind of the Spirit, because the Spirit intercedes for the saints according to the will of God.

Can our hope be self-deception? How do we know that when we hope for "what we do not see" our hope will not be disappointed? The answer to this question is certainly not that we simply hope and trust to the future, an undefined future. When we trust in the Spirit by whom we are "led" (verse 14), our hope is not aimless but "according to the will of God" (verse 27). This trust in the Spirit given to us as the "spirit of sonship" (verse 15) and the "first fruits" (verse 23), is required of us because "we do not know how to pray as we ought" and "the Spirit himself intercedes for us."

This does not make prayer for the Christian something superfluous, but gives it a deeper meaning as trust in the Spirit. In prayer we can bring the meaning and the distress of our existence before God; our faith gives us the courage to put all our hope in God and his grace. But to enable us in our prayer, in our longing and hope, to let God be completely God, to rely in our expectations in life only on this God who justifies and bestows holiness, and not to turn to any substitute god, for this we need the Spirit who helps us in our weakness and intercedes for us with "sighs too deep for words," which include not only the groans and the longing of creation but also its not always completely conscious hope. Our hope thus attains in the mind of the Spirit its real certainty.

[28]*We know that everything works for good with those who love God and are called according to his purpose.* [29]*For those whom he foreknew he also predestined to be conformed to the image of his Son, in order that he might be the first-born among many brethren.* [30]*And those whom he predestined he also called; and those whom he called he also justified; and those whom he justified he also glorified.*

The certainty of our hope allows us to bear the "sufferings of this present time" with patience. Whatever we have to face, we have the certainty that "everything works for good" with us. This does not mean that for the Christian nothing is any longer quite so bad as it otherwise appears, or that he has an easier time in his sufferings and distress than others. No, sufferings, even when they are integrated into the Christian's hope, are still sufferings. Christian hope does not allow us to take them lightly, as spiritual enthusiasts have so often deluded people into thinking. Paul is not preaching a Stoic indifference to our experience of suffering on earth, but the certainty of hope in the midst of suffering.

This certainty is reinforced in verse 28 from two aspects. It is the certainty of those "who love God" and are "called" according to God's merciful purpose. The fact that we love God is not our reward or our achievement, not even the result of our own inclinations or goodwill, but "God's love poured into our hearts" (5:5), the love with which God "helps our weakness" (verse 26) and which becomes in us the position of "children of God" (verses 16–17) which survives everything. Those who love God are none other than those whom God has called in his assisting and all-embracing will to save. Verses 29–30 now show in the form of a syllogism how God has worked out his call and brought it to fruition.

The individual members of the syllogism are related to each other in such a way as to describe God's single act of salvation to men in its various aspects. Dogmatic speculation in its search for a Pauline doctrine of predestination has sometimes obscured this central emphasis. The starting point is God's call, addressed to men through Jesus Christ (verses 28, 30). This call is part of Christian faith and finds its response in life " according to the Spirit." God's call has universal effect, just as faith is universal, insofar as men really respond to the call which reaches them and so attain faith.

Concluding Praise of "God for Us" (8:31–39)

31 What then shall we say to this? If God is for us, who is against us? 32 He who did not spare his own Son, but gave him up for us all, will he not also give us all things with him?

The certainty of faith and hope finally reaches a climax in verse 31 with a joyful cry of victory: " God is for us!" With this exclamation Paul seems to have forgotten his reminders about the " sufferings of this present time " and the demands of life in hope. In reality, though, neither excludes the other; the fact that " we love God " and so respond to the call we have received is simply inconceivable and impossible without the God who revealed himself as " God for us " by giving up his son " for us all " in his love. The cry of victory " God for us " is often misunderstood and misused egoistically. Which " holy " war has not called on the God " on our side "? But " God for us " is the God of those who hope " in patience " (verse 25). This warcry can only be used against the adversary who always has something to say against us before God, which means against God's saving actions, who tries to play God off against himself. But God is one, " God for us."

[33]*Who shall bring any charge against God's elect? It is God who justifies;* [34]*who is to condemn? Is it Christ Jesus, who died, yes, who was raised from the dead, who is at the right hand of God, who indeed intercedes for us?*

The charge against the " elect of God " founders on God himself. Christians' awareness of themselves as " God's elect " is justified by the rest of the account of salvation in this chapter. They have really attained salvation, have received the " spirit of sonship " and are now " children of God "; they have a title to the promise of " future glory," and God " will give them all things " in Christ who died and was raised for them; they have now begun to love God, and can justly call themselves " God's elect." Only when all the elements of this description are taken seriously can the Christian consciousness of election avoid the taint of Pharisaical presumption and complacency and show its genuineness in a hope that shares the concern of God's saving activity for all mankind.

The basis of our assurance of salvation is here once again revealed as God's justifying acts, which leave all condemnation of sin behind. The question in verse 34 silences all who wanted to bring charges. The silence is broken by the cry "Christ Jesus!" This cry is the cry of salvation, the appeal to the saviour against the condemnatory accusation of the opponents of salvation. Christ Jesus, which means the Jesus who died for us, was raised, exalted to the right hand of God and who intercedes for us. Christ Jesus is for us not the past, but present and future.

³⁵*Who shall separate us from the love of Christ? Shall tribulation, or distress, or persecution, or famine, or nakedness, or peril, or sword?* ³⁶*As it is written,*

   "For thy sake we are being killed all the day long;
   we are regarded as sheep to be slaughtered."

³⁷*No, in these things we are more than conquerors through him who loved us.* ³⁸*For I am sure that neither death nor life, nor angels, nor principalities, nor things present, nor things to come, nor powers,* ³⁹*nor height, nor depth, nor anything else in all creation, will be able to separate us from the love of God in Christ Jesus our Lord.*

So at the end the confession of faith leads us back to Christ Jesus, with a passing glance at all the " sufferings of this present time," the extent of which is underlined by a quotation from Ps. 44:23, to a hymn which proclaims the certainty of present and future hope. It is a hymn in praise of God's love, which he has revealed to us in Christ Jesus and which the apostle knows is the source of the salvation of the world. Unshakable adherence to this love of his makes our existence " more than victorious," because through the conformity of our believing existence with the love of God, and only through that, all the powers and forces which oppose us will be overcome.

By clinging to this union with God, we prove our freedom, for which we were set free (cf. verse 2), to be freedom from " slavery to transitoriness " and obtain in reality the " glorious liberty of the children of God."

Israel
(9:1—11:36)

In the context of the letter as a whole, chapters 9 to 11 look at first sight like a switch to a quite different subject: Paul is discussing the fate of Israel. This question arises for him directly from the proclamation of the message of justification, and this is the link which joins these three " Israel chapters " to the main theme of the letter.

What is the significance of Israel, if everything depends on Christ and no longer on the law? We are told that Christ is " the end of the law " (10:4). But Israel has not been converted; arguably she has remained true to her special election by God and by so doing has forfeited in the present the goal of that historical election. Paul is here using the concept of election in an attempt to understand how Israel has excluded herself from " God's righteousness," which has now been made manifest, and tried to establish her own righteousness instead (10.3). God's election has come to fruition in the present in the universal Church made up of Jews and Gentiles. Nevertheless this election remains directed to the historical Israel. This tension of simultaneous election and rejection has to be taken seriously in all three chapters, since it is in this that Paul hopes to find an answer to the problem of " Israel."

Chapters 9 to 11 are therefore not a digression, but a final development, from the point of view of historical theology, of the single subject of " the gospel for Jews and Gentiles." Israel too must be converted, must become converted to the way of the " Gentiles "; she must include herself among the needy in order to be saved.

Election in Israel (9:1–29)

Anguish for Israel (9 :1–5)

¹I am speaking the truth in Christ, I am not lying; my conscience bears me witness in the Holy Spirit, ²that I have great sorrow and unceasing anguish in my heart. ³For I could wish that I

*myself were accursed and cut off from Christ for the sake of
my brethren, my kinsmen by race. ⁴They are Israelites, and to
them belong the sonship, the glory, the covenants, the giving of
the law, the worship, and the promises; ⁵to them belong the
patriarchs, and of their race, according to the flesh, is the Christ,
who is God over all blessed for ever. Amen.*

The question Paul is about to discuss obviously affects him
deeply. The question of Israel, its relationship to Christ, its
history and its future, is a personal matter for him. Before he can
even formulate it, and before he has even mentioned Israel, he
expresses his sorrow and anguish over this people as a personal
grief. They are his " brethren," members of his own people. For
their sake he is prepared to give up his most precious possession,
his connection with Christ, if it would win them for Christ. This
readiness recalls Moses' words to God when he interceded for
the people after they had made themselves " gods of gold ":
" But now, if thou wilt forgive their sin—and if not, blot me, I
pray thee, out of thy book which thou has written " (Ex. 32 : 32).
Naturally neither Paul's attitude nor Moses' prayer should be
understood as an attempt to bargain with God. God's actions
are higher than men's thoughts and wishes, even if his grace is
always active in human prayer, longing and compassion for their
fellows and such compassion among men is always part of
God's compassion. Paul's love for his people is evident, and his
worry and anger at their refusal to accept Christ is eloquent
testimony to it.

God's Faithfulness to His Promise in the History of Israel (9 :6–13)

*⁶But it is not as though the word of God had failed. For not all
who are descended from Israel belong to Israel, ⁷and not all are
children of Abraham because they are his descendants; but
" Through Isaac shall your descendants be named." ⁸This means
that it is not the children of the flesh who are the children of
God, but the children of the promise are reckoned as descen-*

dants. *⁹For this is what the promise said, " About this time I will return and Sarah shall have a son."*

In verse 6 Paul deals with a possible objection which is not raised explicitly and which throws doubt on God's faithfulness to his promise. If all that has just been said about the distinctive honors of Israel is justified, should we not expect proof of this in the present in God's faithfulness to his word? Paul answers the objection with an incident from Yahweh's history with his people. This shows that promise and fulfillment always depend on the free choice of the power of God's grace. By his promises God binds himself to human history, but without allowing his freedom of action to be narrowed or determined by men's expectations. This must be recognized as a feature of Israel's history, which is a history of promise, election and fulfillment. God's mighty acts in the history of Israel have always been directed, not at " Israel according to the flesh " (1 Cor. 10 : 18), but at " the Israel of God " (Gal. 6 : 16). This is summed up in verse 6b : " for not all who are descended from Israel belong to Israel." This is not playing off one Israel against another, but a way of stressing that throughout the history of Israel God was at work choosing and leading his own Israel.

There is at least some justification for taking this passage as saying that the Church is the " true Israel." Certainly the Church of those who believe in Christ which exists in the present is included in the action of God's choice, but what Paul has directly in mind is the Israel of the history of covenant and promise to which scripture witnesses. It is in and through this history that God reveals himself as the God of " his Israel." It is in this light that we should also understand the following verses.

External descent from Abraham does not mean that his bodily descendants are all really his " children " (9 : 7). This idea is found many times in the New Testament, beginning with the preaching of John the Baptist (cf. Mt. 3 : 9; Lk. 3 : 8; Jn. 8 : 33, 37-47, 52-59; Rom. 4; Gal. 3). Verse 9 : 8 explains what " children " really means. Paul first illustrates the challenging statement in 9:7 with an example from the Old Testament's own contrast of the two sons of Abraham. The fact that God's choice fell on Isaac and that in this way " Abraham's seed " was transmitted only through Isaac, is entirely God's affair (cf. the contrast between Abraham's two wives, Sarah and Hagar, in Gal. 4:21–31). We cannot go behind this choice to find purely historical reasons for it, and this indicates that " God's history " is not simply identical with history, even though it constantly takes place within our human history.

The result of this unity in tension between God's historical captivity and objective history is expressed in verse 8: " it is not the children of the flesh who are the children of God, but the children of the promise—and Paul ends the sentence slightly unexpectedly—" are reckoned as descendants." The " children of the flesh " and the " children of the promise " are contrasted; between them stands the action of God's choice. The question which now presents itself—Is God just to do this?—is for the most part held over, to be dealt with explicitly in verse 14. Part of the answer, however, is in verse 8, which tells us that the " children of God " owe their position entirely to God's choice. It is completely a matter for God who is " reckoned " as a " descendant " of Abraham.

[10]*And not only so, but also when Rebecca had conceived children by one man, our forefather Isaac, [11]though they were not yet born and had done nothing either good or bad, in order that God's purpose of election might continue, not because of works but because of his call, [12]she was told, " The elder will serve the younger." [13]As it is written, " Jacob I loved, but Esau I hated."*

Paul follows one example with another. The history of Israel provides him with the necessary material. But again with this example the reader is not meant to ponder the " how " or " why "; the parenthesis in verse 11 makes clear what is the real point.

Here again two sons are contrasted. The relationships are rather different from those of the first example: we start not with two mothers, but with a single father and a single mother. And the sons of Rebecca and Isaac are twins, which only sharpens the statement of God's election. Even more strongly this time than before, it is emphasized that none of the considerations that operate in human history can determine God's choice. Verse 11a emphasizes further the free action of God's choice: they were not yet born and had done nothing either good or bad—this was the position in which the word of God's promise came to Rebecca (verse 12).

In God's actions and plans his free choice must be taken seriously (verses 11b–12). This action of election itself leads to a goal, which is ultimately salvation as a gift of God and which involves the fulfillment of the history of his people. Paul indeed does not here make explicit this implication of his argument, though in view of verse 6 we must remember that God by his word has bound himself to Israel, and that the subject of the present discussion is "Israel" and not the "providence" of God or the freedom of his actions. But this underlying question of "Israel" cannot be solved separately from the "theology of justification," as the remark "not because of works" in verse 12 indicates. This is made even clearer in what follows.

In verse 13 the idea of election is formulated a last time in a way that arouses our natural human feelings, in a text of Scripture: "Jacob I loved, but Esau I hated" (Mal. 1:2–3). Paul sees the stress of the statement as lying on the free election of God as shown in his actions. But God's freedom does not consist in showing love here and hate there, but in the fact that he himself is where he bestows his love. This is the experience of God's gracious approach in Christ.

God's freedom in Creating the new People of God (9:14–29)

God's Creative Power and Election (9:14–21)

¹⁴*What shall we say then? Is there injustice on God's part? By*

no means! ¹⁵*For he says to Moses, " I will have mercy on whom I will have mercy, and I will have compassion on whom I will have compassion." ¹⁶So it depends not upon man's will or exertion, but upon God's mercy. ¹⁷For the Scripture says to Pharaoh, " I have raised you up for the very purpose of showing my power in you, so that my name may be proclaimed in all the earth."*

Paul keeps adding points to bring out all the aspects of the " Israel problem." Even where he seems to be going into subsidiary questions, as in the present section (verses 14–17), he never loses sight of the main problem. It is clear that there is no short formula to include all the aspects of the question, any more than there is any easy solution. The crucial starting point for any solution has, however, already been indicated : God elects, disposes and acts according to his freedom, which has its origin within him, and this is illustrated in the history of Israel by the fact that what Israel is and will be depends on God alone.

Given this assumption, the objection of the questioner in verse 14 must be simply rejected. " Injustice on God's part " is a self-contradictory concept. God's righteousness is revealed in the very fact that he acts as he does. Paul illustrates this by a saying of Yahweh's to Moses, " I will have mercy on whom I will have mercy . . ." " God's righteousness " is revealed by the fact that in showing mercy he has no origin outside himself, he is really himself. God reveals himself as God in the fact that no one can assist him by " will " or " exertion."

If the Old Testament gave Paul a " positive " example of the free action of God in verse 15, it gives him a " negative " example in verse 17. God " showed his power " in Pharaoh in a way that strikingly transcended all human power. Even in Pharaoh's plans against the people of God, God is active, active in order that he can be recognized as himself.

¹⁸*So then he has mercy on whomever he wills, and he hardens the heart of whomever he wills.*

This sentence must not be divorced from its context. If it is, it may be misunderstood and taken to imply a dark, impenetrable predestination of human salvation and damnation. God's free election in his saving activity can be so totally misunderstood that what is ultimately the reign of God and the salvation of man appears to man as arbitrariness and blind fate. God attains his end, and this is the basis of man's salvation.

The nature of God's free election in his activity was described in the preceding examples from Old Testament history, lastly in the saying to Moses (verse 15) and the saying to Pharaoh (verse 17). The two sayings show both the merciful and the hardening action of God. These examples are overshadowed, however, by the present, in which God's activity is experienced with a new clarity. God's compassion on whomever he will has been confirmed in the present by the new people of God called into existence by God. And on the other side—in spite of verses 1–5 Paul cannot deny it—the claims and merit of Israel have revealed themselves as a hardening against God's saving action in Christ, with the result that God's election once more as before in the history of his people (cf. 9:7f., 10), splits the visible Israel in order to create his own Israel.

[19]*You will say to me then, " Why does he still find fault? For who can resist his will? " [20]But who are you, a man, to answer back to God? Will what is moulded say to its moulder, " Why have you made me thus? " [21]Has the potter no right over the clay, to make out of the same lump one vessel for beauty and another for menial use?*

The objection from verse 14 is repeated in a modified form. If God then predetermines everything and even brings about the hardening, how can he still find fault? Surely a man can do nothing in the face of God's disposition; the man whose heart has been hardened cannot defend himself against God—is not a " higher will " at work in him? The picture of God threatens to assume diabolical features. Who can resist God's will? Indeed, no one can resist him. But in that case how does it happen that man can mistake the will of God and resist it? Paul gives no direct answer to these questions. Obviously all of them, humanly so understandable, are here meant only to throw light on God's Godhead from man's point of view, which, according to verses 20f., means to let the creature see the creator in his true light.

The New People of God Includes Both Jews and Gentiles (9 :22–29)

[22]*What if God, desiring to show his wrath and make known his power, has endured with much patience the vessels of wrath made for destruction,* [23]*in order to make known the riches of his glory for the vessels of mercy, which he has prepared beforehand for glory . . . ?*

Verses 22–23 form an incomplete question, but even without the missing answer the point is clear. In the face of history, which in fact unfolds in accordance with God's plan, all the theoretical objections of human critics fail. Not even the severest critic can continue to challenge God's predetermining and elective action when he sees that the revelation of wrath in the " vessels of wrath " is not arbitrary—its purpose is to " show his power " but not in an arbitrary way—and that God's ultimate concern is the saving revelation of his glory in the " vessels of mercy." In the interest of this revelation of salvation God has " endured with much patience " the vessels of wrath " made for destruction." In this passage we see the idea of predestination being absorbed into the present experience of the merciful love of God and so losing its character of grim inevitability. God's mercy has been revealed in the present as the creative power with which he formed the new People of God out of both Jews and Gentiles. The very ones who seemed lost, the children of wrath, have become children of his mercy. In this new creative act God's freedom of choice has now revealed itself as merciful election.

Paul's argument here implies that the present is more than simply an extension of the history from which the earlier examples of election were taken. The Christian present is not just another period of history, but the revealed present of the God of election, who creates his own Israel out of both Jews and Greeks.

[24]. . . *even us whom he has called, not from the Jews only but also from the Gentiles.*

God has called us; we are " the vessels of mercy." In these words Paul addresses the Christian community in Rome, and includes with them himself and all who believe in Christ. God's creative call has reached " us," who respond to the call in faith. Jews and Gentiles have been affected by the call which went out in the gospel—" not from the Jews only but also from the Gentiles." In this way God has found the vessels of his mercy among the vessels of wrath. He chooses them freely, but his choice is not made in simple historical continuity with the old Israel; on the contrary, it is by breaking apart the history of the old Israel in favor of a new universal Israel. It was for the sake of the un-restricted universality of God's saving action that the old Israel had to be broken open in order to achieve its true form in the " Israel of God."

In this passage Paul is using the Old Testament idea of the People of God to illuminate the problem of Israel. We find that a solution of the problem raised by the history of election in Israel will not be found simply in a consideration of the history of election, but in the contrast between Israel and the Church, between the old People of God and the new.

[25]*As indeed he says in Hosea,*
  " *Those who were not my people*
  I will call ' my people,'
  and her who was not beloved
  I will call ' my beloved.' "
[26]" *And in the very place where it was said to them,*
  ' *You are not my people,'*
  they will be called ' sons of the living God.' "
    [27]*And Isaiah cries out concerning Israel: " Though the num-*

*ber of the sons of Israel be as the sand of the sea, only a rem-
nant of them will be saved;* [28]*for the Lord will execute his sentence upon the earth with rigor and dispatch."*

[29]*And as Isaiah predicted,*
" If the Lord of hosts had not left us children,
*we would have fared like Sodom and been made like
Gomorrah."*

Verses 25–29 give the scriptural backing for the assertion in
verse 24. In conclusion Paul is able to show from Scripture itself
that even under the Old Covenant God's saving action already
envisaged a new creation of Israel. If the question is asked,
whether, in the light of the new situation between Israel and the
Church, God's word of promise to Israel has not "failed"
(verse 6), then the answer must be a quotation such as Hos.
2 : 1 : " Those who were not my people I will call 'my people,'
and her who was not beloved I will call 'my beloved.' " This
prophetic announcement, incredible to Jewish ears, shows what
election by God is. It is a call which brings forth life. God is
the one " who calls into existence the things that do not exist "
(4 : 17). The second quotation from Hosea is to be taken in the
same way. There is no need to ask which place and which
people the prophet meant at the time, or whether he only
meant this saying to shock Israel into understanding. The truth
is that the Old Testament sayings only receive their full force
when they are read and understood in the light of the Christ-
event of the present. It is in the Christian present that the word
of promise reveals its real scope; we can even say that it is only
in the present determined by the Christ-event that it can be
discovered as a word of promise.

The two quotations from Isaiah which end the section refer
particularly to Israel in the present. " The remnant " of the old
Israel is taken up into the new People of God. In this way God
fulfills " the word," but this fulfillment is not a literal fulfillment of an old promise—in fact the sayings of the prophets had
already indicated that God accomplishes his purpose in such a

way that the history of his people inevitably involves "rigor and dispatch" (verse 28).

Against this background the problem of "Israel" is now restated. The "remnant" is the starting point, but not the end of God's actions.

Israel's Guilt Inexcusable (9:30—10:21)

Paul sums up the conclusions of the previous section. The new People of God consisting of Jews and Gentiles is a reality which calls in question the existence of the old Israel at its root. What is Israel to do now, if its zeal for God and the law and the constant striving for righteousness this involved is after all to be annulled by the action of God's election? Israel cannot accept the claim that Christ is the end of the law (10:4) without giving up its *raison d'être*. This is the core of the problem: Israel cannot remain what it is, but must become the "Israel of God." Instead of relying on its own righteousness it must rely on God's. Putting the position in this way makes it clear that Paul is approaching the problem of Israel from the point of view of the message of justification, and this at the same time throws his preaching of justification into new and sharper relief.

The "Stumbling Stone" (9:30–33)

[30]*What shall we say, then? That Gentiles who did not pursue righteousness have attained it, that is, righteousness through faith;* [31]*but that Israel who pursued the righteousness which is based on law did not succeed in fulfilling that law.* [32]*Why? Because they did not pursue it through faith, but as if it were based on works. They have stumbled over the stumbling stone,* [33]*as it is written:*

"*Behold, I am laying in Zion a stone that will make men stumble,*

a rock that will make them fall;

and he who believes in him will not be put to shame."

God's elective action has brought about a situation in which the new People of God includes both Jews and Gentiles, and is thereby a symbol of the universality of God's saving actions. This statement is of great importance with regard to all Israel, both as seen in the present and in its faithfulness to the old Covenant. This becomes particularly clear when Israel takes its stand against all the world on its own essence, on its law. The result is that the Gentiles who do not possess the law, and who "did not pursue righteousness" have attained it (v. 30). Israel, on the other hand, which possessed the law which promised righteousness, and "pursued" it, did not attain its goal (v. 31). With God "pursuing" and "exertion" (v. 16) are of no importance, only God himself and his call. This call must be heard, and it cannot be heard in an inherited law or a claim based on that, but only in faith.

That the Gentiles attain righteousness and not Israel is not the irony of fate, not simply an arbitrary disruption of the situation, but God's disposition. God has laid down the "stone of stumbling," that is to say, Christ. Israel stumbled against Christ. The "stone to make men stumble" and the "rock to make men fall" (v. 33, quoting Is. 8:14) laid by God has become at the same time the doom of Israel and the basis of salvation for the Gentile world. Israel made its decision at the coming of Christ, with the result that it did not attain righteousness "because they did not pursue it through faith, but as if it were based on works" (verse 32). It is this critical force of the Christ-event, the scandal of the cross (1 Cor. 1:23) which becomes visible in Israel. When Paul in chapter 10 uses the message of justification to elucidate the problem of Israel, he is using it as the kerygmatic expression of the Christ-event.

Self-Righteousness (10:1–3)

¹*Brethren, my heart's desire and prayer to God for them is that they may be saved. ²I bear them witness that they have a zeal for God, but it is not enlightened. ³For, being ignorant of the righteousness that comes from God, and seeking to establish their own, they did not submit to God's righteousness.*

As a people, Israel refused to believe in the salvation which appeared in Christ. Nevertheless, or indeed all the more urgently for that reason, Paul hopes and prays that all Israel may be "saved." He can bear witness from his own experience that his brothers in Israel have "zeal for God," genuine religion and a sincere willingness to do all that the law requires to achieve righteousness before God. Paul's testimony to his fellow Jews here is a warning against facile judgments on hypocrisy in Jewish piety and obedience to the law. It is a superficial reading of the New Testament which regards a purely external commitment to God and one's fellow men, rather than a true dedication, as the actual position of most Jews. Certainly the Pharisees and scribes appear in the gospels with the priestly aristocracy as the sworn enemies of Jesus, but we should remember that the hostile attitude of the upper circles of Jewish society to Jesus represents the attitude of mankind as a whole towards the revelation which took place in Christ. This of course is not to deny the strict religious practice of the Jews could give an impression of posturing and legalism and risked being trapped in complacency.

Paul qualifies his words about Israel's zeal by adding that it is not enlightened. They rely on the law and think that this tells them all they need to know about the will of God (cf. 2:17f.). They saw their duty as being to keep the will of God as found in the law in order to attain righteousness. But by so doing they became "ignorant of the righteousness that comes from God" which was offered to them in Jesus Christ. Here lies Israel's guilt. To be ignorant of God's righteousness and not to acknowledge God's definitive offer of salvation in Christ means to refuse glory to God and to rely on one's "own" acquired righteousness rather than on the God who reveals himself.

Jesus Christ himself is the manifestation of "God's righteousness" (cf. 1:27; 3:21). He forces a decision. He must be obeyed in faith. Anything else, any form of refusal or excuse, is self-righteousness, the insistence on the supremacy of one's own ego. When "I" prescribe the form in which God must reveal himself, God is no longer revealing himself, but man's ego is putting itself in the place of God and his eschatological revelation. This human self-assertion is active even in what may appear to be faithfulness to God's covenant promises. If Israel's faithfulness consists only in faithfulness to tradition and the promises handed down as part of that tradition, they run the risk of not recognizing God's eschatological revelation and disobeying it when it appears. Israel's failure lay in their lack of this willingness to meet God in the way he wishes to reveal himself in the present and future.

The New Righteousness (10:4–13)

⁴For Christ is the end of the law, that everyone who has faith may be justified. ⁵Moses writes that the man who practices the righteousness which is based on the law shall live by it. ⁶But the righteousness based on faith says, Do not say in your heart, "Who will ascend into heaven?" (that is, to bring Christ down) ⁷or "Who will descend into the abyss?" (that is, to bring Christ up from the dead). ⁸But what does it say? The word is near you, on your lips and in your heart (that is, the word of faith which we preach).

Israel, which places such value on "righteousness" before God, has passed righteousness by. The new righteousness, which has been made manifest in Christ and so accessible in faith to "everyone," requires from the historical Israel the complete abandonment of its own efforts towards righteousness. It requires as part of this the setting aside of the law and reliance through faith on Christ. In a short, exact phrase Christ appears as "the end of the law," of the path of the law which Israel has followed hitherto and of the righteousness built thereon. Christ is also the end of the old Israel which lived by the law and understood itself in terms of the law. He is its end because he is the beginning of the new Israel, already visible as the "Israel of God" in the universal community of believers which includes both Jews and Gentiles.

Two versions of righteousness are opposed in the problem of

Israel, the righteousness "based on the law" (verse 5) and the righteousness "based on faith" (verse 6). The two are opposed —but not as two possibilities between which to choose. The righteousness based on the law is no longer a real possibility; the righteousness based on faith has made it impossible. So even Moses' testimony quoted from Lev. 18:5 with reference to the righteousness based on the law can only confirm the principle of works which is at the heart of the path of the law; it cannot demonstrate that the path of the law is a present possibility. Even this testimony thus becomes indirectly (and not just because no man does or could in fact fulfil the law) testimony in support of the new righteousness based not on works of the law but on faith in Christ. Christ cannot be replaced by any human efforts; put in another way, he cannot be "brought down" from heaven (verse 6) or "brought up" from the "abyss" (verse 7). The Old Testament quotations which Paul uses are always given an exegetical extension which illustrates very clearly his method of interpreting scripture (i.e., the Old Testament) constantly with reference to Christ.

[9] *. . . because, if you confess with your lips that Jesus is Lord and believe in your heart that God raised him from the dead, you will be saved.* [10]*For man believes with his heart and so is justified, and he confesses with his lips and so is saved.* [11]*The scripture says, " No one who believes in him will be put to shame."*

At the center of the faith preached by Paul, which was also, and even "first" addressed to Israel (cf. 1:16), stands Jesus Christ. In phrases which echo the creeds, and sometimes clearly in close reliance on a previously existing creed, Paul reveals faith in Jesus as saving faith. The concluding scripture text in verse 13 makes Israel's Covenant formula witness to the universal Christian faith.

The subject of the creed is Jesus as the *Kyrios*, the Lord. Faith means accepting Jesus as Lord and submitting permanently to his rule. Chapter 6 has already shown us that this is a requirement which involves the whole of life. But faith also means accepting set formulas which elaborate the basic confession of faith in the Lord Jesus, in this case in particular "that God raised him from the dead." The raising of Jesus is the basic content and—rightly understood—the root of the Christian creed, because in and with Christ God has raised us to life, to the life we now possess in faith, faith which hopes but does not yet see (cf. 8:24). In raising Jesus from the dead God showed his creative power, and it is to this power of God which creates things anew that we have to submit, so that salvation may be revealed as God's "new creation."

¹²*For there is no distinction between Jew and Greek; the same Lord is Lord of all and bestows his riches upon all who call upon him.* ¹³*For, " every one who calls upon the name of the Lord will be saved."*

With all the clarity one could wish for Paul once more stresses the universality of the new righteousness inaugurated in Christ. He does it with a reference to the universal scope of God's rule: "The same Lord is Lord of all." Israel must come to understand this one universal lordship in order to attain salvation. Under this one lordship there is "no distinction" any longer between Jews and Gentiles. This makes salvation history a problem, as the very existence of Israel is a problem. As God's chosen people, Israel had constantly to bear in mind its distinctiveness from the Gentile world—what other meaning could its election have? In Christ it is made clear that the only possible meaning of election is that human expectations, and even Israel's expectations and ideas of righteousness are transcended by God himself, who calls all men without distinction. The absence of distinctions in the attainment of salvation includes the absence of distinctions in sin: "all have sinned and fall short of the glory of God " (3:23). So Israel finally has no choice but to turn to this one Lord.

No Excuse for Israel (10:14–21)

¹⁴*But how are men to call upon him in whom they have not*

believed? And how are they to believe in him of whom they have never heard? And how are they to hear without a preacher? ¹⁵*And how can men preach unless they are sent? As it is written, " How beautiful are the feet of those who preach good news."* ¹⁶*But they have not all heeded the gospel; for Isaiah says, " Lord, who has believed what he has heard from us?"* ¹⁷*So faith comes from what is heard, and what is heard comes from the preaching of Christ.*

Everything depends on the word of God which goes forth and comes to men in the gospel. This word must be heard. God's work reaches its fulfillment in faithful hearing and acceptance of the gospel. This raises the question whether in Israel's case the making present of the word in the gospel ever took place. If not, there would be an excuse for Israel. Paul, however, can take it for granted that the gospel was also—and indeed " first " (1 : 16)—preached to the Jews. The emphasis with which he now explains the process of the word's being made present in the gospel only stresses further Israel's lack of success.

¹⁸*But I ask, have they not heard? Indeed they have; for " Their voice has gone out to all the earth, and their words to the ends of the world."*

Israel has heard, because the gospel has gone out " to all the earth." This quotation from the psalms (Ps. 19:4) does not refer in its original context to the gospel as " the preaching of Christ " (verse 17), but to the works of creation in which God reveals himself. Paul can relate this process of revelation celebrated in an Old Testament psalm to the gospel without undue violence to its sense because all the previously uttered " words " of God find their true and final meaning in the gospel. This is why Paul says that the sound of the gospel has gone out to all the earth. It is destined for the whole world, and in the preaching of the Apostle it is in the process of going round the earth, as far as Rome and beyond. But Israel still has not attained faith, and that is the basis of its guilt before God.

[19]Again I ask, did Israel not understand? First Moses says,
  " I will make you jealous of those who are not a nation;
  with a foolish nation I will make you angry."
[20]Then Isaiah is so bold as to say,
  " I have been found by those who did not seek me:
  I have shown myself to those who did not ask for me."
[21]But of Israel he says, "All day long I have held out my hands
to a disobedient and contrary people."

What more does Israel need? They have heard the gospel. Do they only lack understanding? But Israel above all ought to be the first to understand, since they boast of understanding the will of God and what a relationship with God entails (cf. 2:18). But it is apparent that it is not this presumed understanding that brings men to faith, but God who calls. This can be seen in the call of the Gentiles, the " foolish nation " which was called in spite of having no previous disposition to understand.

In this way Israel's priority in salvation history was broken. God revealed himself to " those who are not a nation," those " who did not seek me, . . . who did not ask for me." God allowed all this to make Israel " jealous," for even now Israel has not been forgotten and abandoned by God. " All day long," including the present, God holds out his hands to his " disobedient and contrary people." Israel's election has not simply lapsed, because the same God of election is also at work in the present. The path of " jealousy " may thus ultimately be the way by which Israel recovers what it has missed in the present.

God's Faithfulness to His Promise to Israel
(11:1–36)

In the present Israel has let salvation pass it by. Has it thereby finally forfeited its election? The question can only be answered by God's word of election itself. Insofar as God is the only source of election, his word will not " fail " (9:6). It is this which still gives Israel a chance: God has not withdrawn his election or his promise to Israel; he has already begun to fulfill the promise in the present, but even in Israel's hardening against him he leaves open the possibility of grace. The original bearer of the promise has not been forgotten in the saving events of the present, but is still, even as an unwilling partner, borne along by the action of God's grace. Even if in the light of the preceding passage Israel's guilt seems enormous, God will nevertheless achieve his purpose in and with Israel as the God of the promise.

The "Remnant" of Israel (11:1-10)

¹I ask, then, has God rejected his people? By no means! I myself am an Israelite, a descendant of Abraham, a member of the tribe of Benjamin. ²ᵃGod has not rejected his people whom he foreknew.

In the Christian present the "Israel question" now appears in the form: "Has God rejected his people?" To admit this would be to draw a false conclusion from the arguments in chapters 9 and 10. Paul does not see Israel as the rejected people of God in contrast to the new people of God accepted in virtue of its faith in Christ. As far as the present is concerned, it can clearly be seen that God has preserved a "remnant" for himself out of Israel, who have entered the new People of God. In this connection Paul can refer in the first instance to himself. He belongs to the people of Israel, as shown by his descent from Abraham and in particular from the tribe of Benjamin.

²ᵇDo you not know what the scripture says of Elijah, how he pleads with God against Israel? ³"Lord, they have killed thy prophets, they have demolished thy altars, and I alone am left, and they seek my life." ⁴But what is God's reply to him? "I have kept for myself seven thousand men who have not bowed the knee to Baal."

What is happening in Israel at present has its prophetic foreshadowing in Elijah and the seven thousand. Elijah was persecuted by Jezebel, the idolatrous wife of King Ahab. In this situation he complained to God about Israel. Israel had become faithless, he alone was left, and now they were seeking his life. God overcame his prophet's doubts. God has "kept" seven thousand men to carry on his plan in Israel. This process is being repeated in the present, or rather, what has now happened in the Israelites who have become believers acquires its particular significance from the fact that God has kept them for himself so that he may be recognized in the present, as in the history of Israel, as the God of election.

[5]*So too at the present time there is a remnant, chosen by grace. [6]But if it is by grace, it is no longer on the basis of works; otherwise grace would no longer be grace.*

What is happening in "the present time" (cf. 3:26) is determined by the elective action of grace in Jesus Christ. The "present time" is therefore the time of salvation in a quite unique way. It is not just time or any time, but the time in which God appears in Jesus Christ and his gospel to bring salvation. This "eschatological" quality also characterizes the "remnant" which God has "kept" for himself (verse 3; cf. 9:27).

It is not by chance that Paul speaks of a "remnant." Contemporary Judaism was well acquainted with the idea of a chosen "remnant" of Israel, especially the apocalyptic groups and movements such as Qumran. The tiny handful in Israel who have believed in Christ can be seen as such a remnant in the present. The emphasis in Paul's usage, however, lies not so much on the saving of the remnant out of the larger Israel doomed to destruction, as on its "election" by God "by grace." This is Paul's understanding of his being a Christian: he is chosen in grace, and that means not by works. He does not parade his Christianity in pharisaical superiority over Israel, but stresses that it is undeserved and the result of election and grace.

But the remnant chosen by God in the present is not in itself the goal of God's saving work. In relation to the total Israel, this remnant appears much more as the current expression of God's elective action. God's goal remains as ever the full number of Israel, as we see more clearly from the following sections.

⁷What then? Israel failed to obtain what it sought. The elect obtained it, but the rest were hardened, ⁸as it is written,
" God gave them a spirit of stupor,
eyes that should not see and ears that should not hear, down
to this very day."
⁹And David says,
" Let their feast become a snare and a trap,
a pitfall and a retribution for them;
¹⁰let their eyes be darkened so that they cannot see,
and bend their backs for ever."

From the chosen " remnant " we turn to Israel as a whole. God's grace has been revealed in " the present time," but Israel in its overwhelming majority has paid no attention to it and held to the principle of works; as a result, judgment has inevitably come upon Israel. Inevitably, because judgment is the other side of grace. Just as grace is associated with election and faith, so is judgment with hardening and works. The chosen remnant becomes a sign of judgment on Israel. Judgment in the present follows the rejection of grace, but it is not a crushing judgment without mercy or grace; on the contrary, election still stands under the present judgment, and grace shines out once more as a hope for the future of Israel. The Old Testament quotations in verses 8–10, however, put the emphasis first on the judgment which has overtaken Israel in the present in the form of " stupor " and " darkness."

The Full Number of Israel (11:11–32)

MAKING ISRAEL JEALOUS (11:11–16)

¹¹So I ask, have they stumbled so as to fall? By no means! But through their trespass salvation has come to the Gentiles, so as to make Israel jealous. ¹²Now if their trespass means riches for the world, and if their failure means riches for the Gentiles, how much more will their full inclusion mean?

Even if the members of the people of Israel have " stumbled " in the present (i.e., on the " stone of stumbling "; cf. 9 : 32ff.), this still does not mean that they have irrevocably " fallen." There is no doubt about their " trespass " in the present, and nothing can be done about it, but even in the present it includes a positive element—through it we see that " salvation has come to the Gentiles." In these verses Paul turns his attention to Israel as a whole, and more precisely to the question of the meaning of the hardening of Israel in relation to the Gentile world. It would be a mistake to see verse 11 as strictly giving a reason for the salvation of the Gentiles, rather than an interpretation of it. Paul certainly does not intend to say that the Gentiles have been saved by the trespass of the Jews, but rather that there is a connection between the hardening of Israel and the acceptance of the Gentiles. This acceptance is of course the result of grace, not works (verse 6), while Israel still clings to works. Yet there is a correlation between Israel and the Gentile world—not merely that salvation has passed Israel by and reached the Gentiles, but also that Israel is made " jealous " by this result of its stubbornness. No doubt Paul is here thinking of his missionary experiences and successes and the reaction of the Jews to them. It is true that the mission among the Gentiles, viewed objectively, led more to a hardening on the part of the Jews than to making them jealous of the Gentiles' salvation. But for Paul the two go together, and he confidently expects that the hardening of Israel will turn more and more into a " holy rivalry."

Verse 12 is a clear statement of Paul's hope, the full number of Israel and its final acceptance by God. This shows that Paul holds to his belief in the election of all Israel, even if he has just spoken of its hardening. It is also the final salvation of Israel which will make clear the relationship which according to verse 11 exists between Israel and the salvation of the whole world; the one thing certain is that it will mean even greater riches for the Gentiles too.

13Now I am speaking to you Gentiles. Inasmuch then as I am an apostle to the Gentiles, I magnify my ministry 14in order to make my fellow Jews jealous, and thus save some of them. 15For if their rejection means the reconciliation of the world, what will their acceptance mean but life from the dead?

Paul now turns explicitly to the Gentiles and the Gentile Christians. The close connection of their salvation with Israel's election imposes a permanent obligation on them with regard to Israel. For the same reasons, Paul does not see his role as " Apostle of the Gentiles," which involves a complete devotion to the Gentile world for their salvation, as a turning away from Israel but as an indirect demand to Israel to follow the example of the Gentiles and attain salvation only through faith in Christ.

16If the dough offered as first fruits is holy, so is the whole lump; and if the root is holy, so are the branches.

Paul rounds off this section by introducing once more the idea of election, in the form of a double parable. Israel's historical election by God does not simply lapse, but remains effective in the present. The first image is taken from the field of worship. Through the offering of first fruits of the year's grain harvest, the whole of the "dough " is sanctified. Paul has here expanded the meaning of the original ceremony as described in Num. 15:17-21. The same holds for the present-day Israel, whose " first fruits," the patriarchs, have made it holy.

The comparison in the second parable does not quite match that in the first. Paul does not say, " if the root is holy, the whole tree is holy," as one might expect, but " the branches are holy." No doubt he is influenced in his descriptions by the image of the olive tree in the following verses. The holiness of the branches connects with the separating, elective character of God's dealings with men, because in Old Testament thought holiness was always seen as being set apart for God. This becomes clearer in the next section, the allegory of the olive tree, into which the mention of the branches leads.

The Wild Olive Tree and the Cultivated Olive Tree (11:17–24)

[17]But if some of the branches were broken off, and you, a wild olive shoot, were grafted in their place to share the richness of the olive tree, [18]do not boast over the branches. If you do boast, remember it is not you that support the root, but the root that supports you. [19]You will say, " Branches were broken off so that I might be grafted in." [20]That is true. They were broken off because of their unbelief, but you stand fast only through faith. So do not become proud, but stand in awe. [21]For if God did not spare the natural branches, neither will he spare you. [22]Note then the kindness and severity of God: severity towards those who have fallen, but God's kindness to you, provided you continue in his kindness; otherwise you too will be cut off.

The allegory of the wild olive and the cultivated olive must be seen in close relation to the problem of Israel as a whole. Paul has brought his readers to a point in his discussion of the question at which there is no longer any doubt, in spite of the hardening of Israel in the present, that this hardening is temporary and that because of God's faithfulness to his promises there is hope even in the hardening. So if the cultivated olive tree, which depends for its existence on God's election, has had some of its " branches " (cf. verse 16) broken off in the present, this is not simply to make room for the branches from the wild olive, but so that God's judgment may be made visible in them, and because God has power to graft them in again (verses 32ff.). This ultimate goal is in Paul's mind even when he begins his argument as a warning to the Gentile Christians not to boast at Israel's expense (verse 18).

The Gentile Christian, in his origin, is a " wild olive tree," in contrast to Israel, the tree which God has planted (Jer. 11:16–17). The Gentile Christian benefits from the richness of the root of Israel (verse 17; cf. verse 16). This relationship between Israel and the Gentile Christians is irreversible, even if branches are broken off from the tree of Israel and God later grafts them in again (verses 23ff.).

²³And even the others, if they do not persist in their unbelief, will be grafted in, for God has the power to graft them in again. ²⁴For if you have been cut from what is by nature a wild olive tree, and grafted, contrary to nature, into a cultivated olive tree, how much more will these natural branches be grafted back into their own olive tree.

When finally those in Israel who have given up their unbelief are grafted in again, their readmission will be due not merely to their original election, but to God, who alone can bring it about. This readmission, which is not just a restoration but a new creation, will show finally that the God of election is, through all the difficulties and discontinuities of Israel's history, the God who is faithful to his promise, whose word does not fail (9:6). Verse 24 ("how much more") lets us see how close to Paul's heart this hope is. And yet Paul also knows that there is only one way to this goal, the life-giving approach of God in grace even to stubborn Israel.

The Mystery of Israel's Salvation (11:25-32)

²⁵Lest you be wise in your own conceits, I want you to understand this mystery, brethren: a hardening has come upon part of Israel, until the full number of the Gentiles come in, ²⁶and so all Israel will be saved; as it is written,
" The Deliverer will come from Zion,
he will banish ungodliness from Jacob";
²⁷" and this will be my covenant with them,
when I take away their sins."

The mystery Paul has to impart is the proper interpretation, inspired by God, of the present hardening of Israel. We have seen from the previous sections that it does not affect all Israel, to the extent that a remnant already confesses saving faith in Christ. But the hardening is also limited in time, "until the full number of the Gentiles come in." Paul can hardly be thinking here of the conversion of the whole world to Christianity, and indeed we may ask whether his words set a definite limit at all, rather than indicating the consecutive relationship between Gentiles and Jews. After the conversion of the Gentiles, which is now in full swing, will come the conversion of Israel (cf. verses 12, 23). There is no mention of either the time or the manner of Israel's salvation. From the point of view of its content, the mystery Paul imparts might well seem disappointing: we learn very little more than Paul has already said in chapter 11. And yet this shows us the true character of the mystery as God's promise. The essential feature of God's revelation is not that it describes the future course of human history in the greatest possible detail and tells us what to expect, but the message that God stands behind this history which itself remains in the darkness of the future. It is true that this disclosure itself brightens the darkness of the future, so that we now see it as God's future and, in faith, certain.

As further proof that God stands behind the future which is revealed to us as a mystery, Paul quotes the words of the " eschatological " prophet, Isaiah, in which God confirms his promise to Israel.

[28]*As regards the gospel they are enemies of God, for your sake; but as regards election they are beloved for the sake of their forefathers. [29]For the gifts and the call of God are irrevocable. [30]Just as you were once disobedient to God but now have received mercy because of their disobedience, [31]so they have now been disobedient in order that by the mercy shown to you they also may receive mercy. [32]For God has consigned all men to disobedience, that he may have mercy upon all.*

Paul is summing up. The problem of Israel as he sees it has two aspects, the gospel and the historical election. In the light of the gospel the People of Israel appear as " enemies " of God because they have rejected his revelation in Christ. But in the light of their own history they appear as beloved by God, and they retain their position in spite of their present rejection of him. The ultimate basis of this conclusion is God himself, who does not revoke his call on the gifts of his grace.

Praise of the Ways of God (11 :33–36)

33*O the depth of the riches and wisdom and knowledge of God! How unsearchable are his judgments and how inscrutable his ways!*
34*" For who has known the mind of the Lord, or who has been his counsellor?"*
35*" Or who has given a gift to him that he might be repaid?"*
36*For from him and through him and to him are all things. To him be glory for ever. Amen.*

Paul ends with a hymn in praise of God's ways. No one can see in advance his plans and actions, and no one by his own efforts can discover his thoughts. But the ways of God have now been revealed, so that the man who relies on his guidance realizes more and more that " everything," the whole of human history, is " from him and through him and to him." By recognizing his lordship, the world attains its final salvation.

Christian Behavior
(12:1—15:13)

The final, so-called " paraenetic " section of the letter illustrates in practical instructions the claim made on believers by the righteousness of God which has now been revealed. Even in this section, however, the central theme of the letter is not forgotten. It is impossible to live as a person justified by God if one does not practice love. The Christian practice of love, which concerns all areas of life, individual and social, is therefore inseparable from justifying faith. In the constantly changing requirements of human life it is an outward sign of God's power.

Christian Life as Service (12:1—13:14)

TRUE WORSHIP (12:1-2)

¹*I appeal to you therefore, brethren, by the mercies of God, to present your bodies as a living sacrifice, holy and acceptable to God, which is your spiritual worship. ²Do not be conformed to this world but be transformed by the renewal of your mind, that you may prove what is the will of God, what is good, acceptable and perfect.*

These two verses form a sort of title to the following section (chapters 12–15). They indicate the attitude in which the individual admonitions which follow are to be understood and put into practice. They state the two basic principles of living a Christian existence: (1) Christian existence means the presentation of " bodies " as a " living sacrifice " and " spiritual worship ": (2) Christian existence has to take account of " this world ": that means that Christians must be on their guard against adapting to the " form " of this passing age, or, in other words, they must transform themselves in a permanent process of renewing their minds so that they become capable of recognizing the will of God. Both parts of this introductory exhortation are, rightly understood, concerned with the world.

Different Gifts, Different Functions (12:3-8)

³*For by the grace given to me I bid every one among you not to think of himself more highly than he ought to think, but to think with sober judgment, each according to the measure of faith which God has assigned him.*

The apostle's advice in the following verses is given in virtue of the grace given to him. Directing the communities is part of his apostolic office. What he has to say to the communities with regard to the practical activities of their lives has therefore an official character; it derives its force from the grace of God by which Paul was called to his ministry. It is the same grace with which God approaches men in mercy (cf. verse 1) and which now becomes active in Paul's advice to the community.

⁴For as in one body we have many members, and all the members do not have the same function, ⁵so we, though many, are one body in Christ, and individually members of one another.

The appeal for sobriety turns out to refer to the relationship of the " members " to each other. Paul has previously used the image of the one body and the many members in a similar context in 1 Cor. 12; it was one which came readily to his lips when he discussed the community and the common activities of its members. He used it to make a number of related points. In Corinth he emphasized the unity of the community amid the diversity of spiritual gifts, whereas here the stress is more on the consideration the members of the community should show to one another, as is indicated by the appeal for personal modesty in verse 3. In recognizing the spiritual gifts which an individual has in the community and for the good of the community, it is important to have a standard for their use. It is necessary to beware of complacency among members of the community about intellectual or spiritual gifts. Such an attitude cannot stem from genuine faith in Jesus Christ.

⁶Having gifts that differ according to the grace given to us, let us use them: if prophecy, in proportion to our faith; ⁷if service, in our serving; he who teaches, in his teaching; ⁸he who exhorts, in his exhortations; he who contributes, in liberality; he who gives aid, with zeal; he who does acts of mercy, with cheerfulness.

The " gifts " or charisms (from *charis*, " grace ") in Paul's list of examples can be seen to be in the main forms of service. Prophecy (cf. 1 Cor. 12 : 10) here does not mean simply oracular utterance but the speech of Christians inspired by God which reveals the truth of things. It is a process involving Christian instruction, exhortation and correction. Prophetic speech always includes a critical attitude to the existing situation, not as a result of a person's own insight and certainly not on principle (criticism for the sake of criticism), but as a result of God's revelation and the insight this gives into the will of God. Christian speech (prophecy) therefore always goes "in proportion to faith," the faith in which the Christian puts himself constantly under the direction of Christ.

Instructions for All (*12:9–21*)

⁹*Let love be genuine; hate what is evil, hold fast to what is good;* ¹⁰*love one another with brotherly affection; outdo one another in showing honor.* ¹¹*Never flag in zeal, be aglow with the Spirit, serve the Lord.* ¹²*Rejoice in your hope, be patient in tribulation, be constant in prayer.* ¹³*Contribute to the needs of the saints, practice hospitality.* ¹⁴*Bless those who persecute you; bless and do not curse them.* ¹⁵*Rejoice with those who rejoice, weep with those who weep.* ¹⁶*Live in harmony with one another; do not be haughty, but associate with the lowly; never be conceited.* ¹⁷*Repay no one evil for evil, but take thought for what is noble in the sight of all.* ¹⁸*If possible, so far as it depends on you, live peaceably with all.* ¹⁹*Beloved, never avenge yourselves, but leave it to the wrath of God; for it is written, " Vengeance is mine, I will repay, says the Lord."* ²⁰*No, " if your enemy is hungry, feed him; if he is thirsty, give him drink; for by so doing you will heap burning coals upon his head."* ²¹*Do not be overcome by evil, but overcome evil with good.*

These are Paul's instructions for correct behavior. It is not easy to see a single theme running through this catalogue of imperatives or a particular arrangement of the individual exhortations. The exhortation to love naturally comes first; it is to be "genuine." In particular, love of the brethren is mentioned (verse 10). Love is the ultimate basis of Christian behavior, as will be stated even more clearly in 13:8–10. Here the outstanding position of love is slightly obscured by its appearance in a list of many exhortations, even if at the head, as one virtue among others, brotherly love.

The Proper Attitude to the Civil Authorities (*13:1–7*)

¹*Let every person be subject to the governing authorities. For there is no authority except God, and those that exist have been*

instituted by God. ²Therefore he who resists the authorities resists what God has appointed, and those who resist will incur judgment. ³For rulers are not a terror to good conduct, but to bad. Would you have no fear of him who is in authority? Then do what is good, and you will receive his approval, ⁴for he is God's servant for your good. But if you do wrong, be afraid, for he does not bear the sword in vain; he is the servant of God to execute his wrath on the wrongdoer. ⁵Therefore, one must be subject, not only to avoid God's wrath but also for the sake of conscience. ⁶For the same reason you also pay taxes, for the authorities are ministers of God, attending to this very thing. ⁷Pay all of them their dues, taxes to whom taxes are due, revenue to whom revenue is due, respect to whom respect is due, honor to whom honor is due.

Is Paul in this section talking particularly about the attitude of Christians to and in the world? Putting the question in this way is a misinterpretation of the text of Romans 13. " World " for Paul is not limited, as it is in our Western tradition, to civil society as opposed to the Church. For Paul it means the total worldly reality, and in particular the human world, as something created and also as a creation which in many ways rejects its creator. Since Christ and because of Christ this world is the old world, into which the new creation has already made an entry. The tension of this existence of a new creation in the declining old world is symbolized by the behavior of the Christian, whose standards are those of the new reality given in Christ. This context should be borne in mind when reading Romans 13 to avoid hasty and facile conclusions from these verses about the Christian attitude to the world.

The admonition on proper behavior towards the civil authorities should not be divorced from the various admonitions which have gone before, though Paul, perhaps for particular reasons, gives the subject special attention.

As in personal relations, so also in relation to the civil authorities, a Christian should " not think of himself more highly than he ought to think" (12:3). Christians have not been simply removed from the visible organization of the state and society; their Christian existence must operate within the given situation. Does this mean a recognition of every form of civil authority, completely without regard to the details of its constitution? Paul's words in verse 1 leave it in no doubt that he recognizes the existing authorities as given by God. He does not ask to what extent the civil authorities themselves recognize their dependence on God or whether in fact they are the manifestation, wholly or in part, of a particular order instituted by God; he simply accepts the existence of governing authorities "instituted by God," while allowing for all possible or likely inadequacies in the exercise of authority. This situation is the Christian's proper starting-point, even if in particular cases he has a duty to judge what the will of God is here and now (12:2). Paul's main concern in this passage, however, is to combat an enthusiasm which, by a misunderstanding of the nature of God's gifts, thinks it can exempt itself from all existing conditions. Paul is a preacher "aglow with the Spirit" (12:11), but not a fanatic, and he calls on Christians to put up with the tension between the existing elements of the world and the share they already possess of the new creation, and not to slacken it.

Love Is the Fulfilling of the Law (13:8–10)

⁸*Owe no one anything, except to love one another; for he who loves his neighbor has fulfilled the law. *⁹*The commandments, "You shall not commit adultery, You shall not kill, You shall not steal, You shall not covet," and any other commandment, are summed up in this sentence, "You shall love your neighbor as yourself." *¹⁰*Love does no wrong to a neighbor; therefore love is the fulfilling of the law.*

In their daily lives, Christians may perform their duties almost as a matter of course, but for all their conscientiousness there remains one duty which is not so easily satisfied, loving one another. Love is a permanent task; it is "the fulfilling of the law." The law cannot be fulfilled by men, and this means that love as the fulfilling of the law is and remains for man, even for the Christian, a goal to strive for. The requirements of the law as instanced in the various commandments are concentrated and given a new force for Christians in the commandment to love. Loving one another is the new Christian possibility, even if it adds nothing new to the demand of Lev. 19:18. The same actions with regard to man and society are performed under this commandment as under the demands of the Old Testament Law, but the intention behind the familiar words of the commandment to love has been given a new definition by Christ's action. The love which Jesus Christ showed in giving his life " for us " (Gal. 2:20) enables us to see our love as the new possibility given by God. The commandment to love, which comes into force anew in Christ's action, directs the Christian towards his neighbor, towards man in the visible world. Love is the way in which Christians bear witness in the world to Christ's action. Love like this is the " bodily worship " for which Paul appealed in his opening words (12:1). Even if it appears in no more than the minimal form of " doing no wrong to a neighbor " (verse 10), it nonetheless constantly opens up in daily life possibilities for " practical worship " which go beyond the " fulfilling of the law."

"You Know What Hour It Is" (13:11–14)

¹¹*Besides this you know what hour it is, how it is full time now for you to wake from sleep. For salvation is nearer to us now than when we first believed; ¹²the night is far gone, the day is at hand. Let us then cast off the works of darkness and put on the armor of light; ¹³let us conduct ourselves becomingly as in the day, not in reveling and drunkenness, not in debauchery and licentiousness, not in quarreling and jealousy. ¹⁴But put on the Lord Jesus Christ, and make no provision for the flesh, to gratify its desires.*

Paul ends by basing his exhortations on the urgency of the last time. Christians know "the time" and realize what hour has come. It is the time in which they now are, marked by the Christ-event and by the moment when they first believed. Yet it is not a time which allows carefree sleep, or resting on the merits of Jesus Christ; it demands vigilance in expectation for the day which will bring the fulfillment of salvation. The imminent arrival of Christ to complete the event of salvation, at whose service as a messenger Paul places himself in the present, is a final decisive motive in Christian life. Because of this Christian behavior is to be recognized by " works " which belong to the day and not to the night. The " works of darkness " can have no longer any place in that day to which Christians look forward, which is already so near that its dawning is no longer in doubt, which has now even begun to dawn and challenge the last domination of darkness.

"Weak" and "Strong" in the One Community (14:1—15:13)

"Do Not Pass Judgment" (14:1-12)

¹*As for the man who is weak in faith, welcome him, but not for disputes over opinions.* ²*One believes he may eat anything, while the weak man eats only vegetables.* ³*Let not him who eats despise him who abstains, and let not him who abstains pass judgment on him who eats; for God has welcomed him.* ⁴*Who are you to pass judgment on the servant of another? It is before his own master that he stands or falls. And he will be upheld, for the Master is able to make him stand.*

In the Christian community in Rome there were tensions between different groups. In earlier sections of the letter we heard of Jewish and Gentile Christians in the one community, and now Paul speaks of " weak " and " strong " in conflict. It is important to notice that the position is described here from the point of view of the " strong," those who took a liberal position on particular questions. They had a keen sense of their freedom, guaranteed to them by Jesus Christ, and sought to maintain their rights in public and by aggressive behavior towards other Christians with different views. Their demonstrative insistence on their freedom incurred condemnation from the others, who on their side held fast to their traditions, and as a result the unity of the community was threatened.

The immediate cause of the tension was whether a Christian could " eat anything " without worrying about whether the meat or wine had been involved in any ritual connected with the pagan Gods. This was probably the reason for the marked reluctance of certain Christians to join in common meals. A similar situation seems to have been the background to 1 Cor. 8:1–13 and 10:14–33. There were Christian enthusiasts in the Corinth community who prided themselves on their " knowledge." By provocative demonstrations that " all things are lawful," they forgot the claims of love and consideration for the " weak " (8:7, 9–12). Paul's experiences with the Corinth community were probably in his mind as he wrote Rom. 14.

In Rome, the " weak " ate no meat at all, but " only vegetables " (verse 2), in order not to incur guilt unawares. Without disputing Christian freedom in any way, Paul first warns the " strong " against arrogance. He then warns those who imposed such restrictions not to judge people with liberal opinions and dismiss them as lawbreakers. He also points out to the " weak " that God has " welcomed " the man they are ready to condemn with moral and theological arguments. It is God's business to judge. The " weak " were tending to usurp his authority as judge, which Paul sees as dangerous because it challenges God's sole power to uphold his " servant," even if he should have fallen.

5One man esteems one day as better than another, while another man esteems all days alike. Let every one be fully convinced in his own mind. 6He who observes the day, observes it in honor of the Lord. He also who eats, eats in honor of the Lord, since he gives thanks to God; while he who abstains, abstains in honor of the Lord and gives thanks to God. ⁷None of us lives to himself, and none of us dies to himself. ⁸If we live, we live to the Lord, and if we die, we die to the Lord; so then, whether we live or whether we die, we are the Lord's. ⁹For to this end Christ died and lived again, that he might be Lord both of the dead and of the living.

Other questions besides food brought out the differences between the two groups. In the " weak " group particular days were observed, perhaps in accord with Jewish practices about sabbaths and fast days. It is not completely clear from Paul's account that Jewish usages are in question here, or that it was in fact Jewish Christians who were the cause of the differences. Various references seem to point to this interpretation (cf. esp. 15 : 8ff.), but in particular it seems likely that Paul would hardly have devoted so much attention to tendencies deriving from Gentile or other sources as he did to residual Jewish elements, provided they offered no serious challenge to Christian freedom.

Paul calls on both groups to be tolerant of each other. " Let every one be convinced in his own mind," and then agreement may be possible. Yet the individual's conviction is based on faith, since everything is done " for the Lord." This for Paul is the decisive argument, that each person in his actions gives thanks to God. If all of them are able to keep their lives directed towards the Lord and keep on developing, this will also preserve the unity of the community. In this way Christ's death and resurrection achieve their object, when he becomes Lord of his community, and is recognized as Lord by all, both " weak " and " strong."

Within the section as a whole verses 7–9 form a unit on their own, with their hymn-like style and the parallelism of living and dying. The use of " we " also (only here in the section) gives the verses a credal character. It looks as though Paul has here used a liturgical text to express the devotion to Christ which brings all the members of the community together.

¹⁰*Why do you pass judgment on your brother? Or you, why do*

you despise your brother? For we shall all stand before the judgment seat of God; ¹¹for it is written,

" As I live, says the Lord, every knee shall bow to me,
and every tongue shall give praise to God."
¹²*So each of us shall give account of himself to God.*

Paul returns to the rhetorical question of verse 4. Since all are equal before the common Lord, judgment among equal brothers is simply impossible. Christians must always behave as brothers towards each other. All judgment is left to God, before whose judgment seat we must all one day appear. Paul underlines the reference to the future judgment with a quotation from Is. 45 : 23.

"Do Not Make Your Brother Stumble" (14 : 13–23)

¹³*Then let us no more pass judgment on one another, but rather decide never to put a stumbling-block or hindrance in the way of a brother. ¹⁴I know and am persuaded in the Lord Jesus that nothing is unclean in itself; but it is unclean for any one who thinks it unclean. ¹⁵If your brother is being injured by what you eat, you are no longer walking in love. Do not let what you eat cause the ruin of one for whom Christ died. ¹⁶So do not let what is good to you be spoken of as evil. ¹⁷For the kingdom of God does not mean food and drink but righteousness and peace and joy in the Holy Spirit; ¹⁸he who thus serves Christ is acceptable to God and approved by men.*

This appeal is directed particularly at the " strong." Christians ought not place obstacles in each other's way, but realize that others are bound in conscience. Even if a Christian is fully justified in saying, " Nothing is unclean in itself," that the old ritual distinction between clean and unclean no longer applies in Christ, this still should not become a hindrance to a brother who still, because he sticks to traditional views, thinks something unclean. The " strong " man must not use his strength as a weapon against the " weak "; this is to act against love. He cannot after all expect the other to be brought to a better understanding by being provoked. As his final reason Paul mentions Jesus' sacrifice of his life; Christ died for all, including the scrupulous. This means that the example of Christ also forbids the " strong " man to allow his " weak " brother to be lost to Christ's saving action by his behavior. He must avoid anything that " injures " his brother.

The question Paul is dealing with is not really a central element of the gospel—that is quite clear. The kingdom of God is certainly not the sort of thing which can be affected by differences of opinion about the permissibility of food and drink. Nevertheless this controversy over practice in a community is relevant to the real point of Christianity. The " kingdom of God " is not an other-worldly and purely transcendent entity beyond our lives; it has already come into being as " righteousness and peace and joy " in the power of the " Holy Spirit," and it is the faith and love of the community which is the most telling evidence for its existence here and now.

[19]*Let us then pursue what makes for peace and for mutual upbuilding.* [20]*Do not, for the sake of food, destroy the work of God. Everything is indeed clean, but it is wrong for any one to make others fall by what he eats;* [21]*it is right not to eat meat or drink wine or do anything that makes your brother stumble.* [22]*The faith that you have, keep between yourself and God; happy is he who has no reason to judge himself for what he approves.* [23]*But he who has doubts is condemned, if he eats because he does not act from faith; for whatever does not proceed from faith is sin.*

Paul continues to speak particularly to the " strong" members of the community. Their behavior should serve the " upbuilding " of the community and not their personal satisfaction. In verse 20 Paul repeats the idea of verse 15: the norm of behavior is the salvation of one's brother. In extreme cases consideration may go so far as to make one abstain from meat or wine in order to avoid giving offense. The " strong " man thus gives up the exercise of his freedom, but not his freedom itself. Freedom is an inalienable possession acquired and preserved by faith in Jesus Christ.

This passage shows clearly that Paul in his preaching does not ignore the salvation of the individual. The central element of his preaching is the " new creation " in Christ as salvation at the end of time for all men. But in the present it is necessary to make every effort to preserve the salvation which has taken root in the believers and bring it to fruition. The " strong " have a particular responsibility here; they are not worried about preserving their own salvation but, perhaps like Paul, see the saving actions of Christ as a comprehensive process which pervades and alters the world. It is important to transmit faithfully these universal implications of the gospel, but this task is only harmed when subjective convictions are thoughtlessly given the status of objective contents of the gospel. The Christian must constantly reassess his knowledge and insights as a believer against the gospel itself.

"Welcome One Another" (15:1–13)

¹We who are strong ought to bear with the failings of the weak, and not to please ourselves; ²let each of us please his neighbor for his good, to edify him. ³For Christ did not please himself; but, as it is written, " The reproaches of those who reproached thee fell on me." ⁴For whatever was written in former days was written for our instruction, that by steadfastness and by the encouragement of the scriptures we might have hope. ⁵May the God of steadfastness and encouragement grant you to live in such harmony with one another, in accord with Christ Jesus, ⁶that together you may with one voice glorify the God and Father of our Lord Jesus Christ.

Paul associates himself with the strong, " we who are strong," and thus supports their appeal to the gospel as the message of Christian freedom. But he goes on to show that the same gospel teaches that Christians are not there to please themselves. On the contrary, each person should please his neighbor, for his

benefit and edification. This follows from the brotherly love
which is the fundamental principle of the Christian community
(cf. 14:15), and it also follows from the example of Christ
himself, who did not seek his own good but took upon himself
the "reproaches" of God's enemies. He denied himself and
became completely selfless in his absolute freedom.

*7Welcome one another, therefore, as Christ has welcomed you,
for the glory of God. 8For I tell you that Christ becomes a servant to the circumcised to show God's truthfulness, in order to
confirm the promises given to the patriarchs, 9and in order that
the Gentiles might glorify God for his mercy. As it is written,*
   *"Therefore I will praise thee among the Gentiles, and sing
   to thy name";*
10and again it is said,
   "Rejoice, O Gentiles, with his people";
11and again,
   "Praise the Lord, all Gentiles,
   and let all the peoples praise him";
12and further Isaiah says,
   "The root of Jesse shall come,
   he who rises to rule the Gentiles;
   in him shall the Gentiles hope."
*13May the God of hope fill you with all joy and peace in believ-
ing, so that by the power of the Holy Spirit you may abound in
hope.*

Paul now sums up his appeal to the community: "Welcome
one another." His appeal is addressed not only to the "strong"
but to both groups. It means in practice that neither group
should exclude the other but accept each other as full members
of the one loving community. The model for such behavior is
Christ, who "welcomed us" as members of the community for
which he gave his life. This single community which includes
"circumcised" and Gentiles is his creation, and created as a
unity, even if the conditions under which Jews and Gentiles
were "welcomed" differ.

CONCLUDING MESSAGES
(15:14-32)

A Restatement of Paul's Reasons for Writing (15:14-21)

¹⁴*I myself am satisfied about you, my brethren, that you your-selves are full of goodness, filled with all knowledge, and able to instruct one another.* ¹⁵*But on some points I have written to you very boldly by way of reminder, because of the grace given me by God,* ¹⁶*to be a minister of Christ Jesus to the Gentiles in the priestly service of the gospel of God, so that the offering of the Gentiles may be acceptable, sanctified by the Holy Spirit.* ¹⁷*In Christ Jesus, then, I have reason to be proud of my work for God.* ¹⁸*For I will not venture to speak of anything except what Christ has wrought through me to win obedience from the Gentiles, by word and deed,* ¹⁹*by the power of signs and wonders, by the power of the Holy Spirit, so that from Jerusalem and as far round as Illyricum I have fully preached the gospel of Christ,* ²⁰*thus making it my ambition to preach the gospel, not where Christ has already been named, lest I build on another man's foundation,* ²¹*but as it is written,*

" They shall see who have never been told of him, and they shall understand who have never heard of him."

At the end of this long and complex letter Paul sets out more explicitly his reasons for writing, as he did in the opening of the letter, 1:8-17. Paul is well aware that it is unusual to write to a community with which he has no previous acquaintance. That is why he says at this point that, of course, the Roman com-munity does not really need instruction from him; indeed, the Christians of Rome are already " full of goodness, filled with all knowledge," and therefore able to give each other instruction and encouragement in their particular situation. But Paul also believes that it is part of his apostolic duty to " remind " communities, even if, as in Rome, they have not been founded by him. The reason for this conviction is that his commission is concerned particularly with the Gentile world. It is among the Gentiles that he wishes to perform his " priestly service " for his gospel, so that the Gentiles may become an acceptable sacrifice (verse 16). Paul understands his preaching of the gospel among the Gentiles as " priestly service "; his aim is to make the Gentiles turn to God and by so doing become a " sacrificial offering," consecrated by the ever-present action of the Spirit of Christ himself.

Paul Announces His Visit (15:22–32)

[22]*This is the reason why I have so often been hindered from coming to you.* [23]*But now, since I no longer have any room for work in these regions, and since I have longed for many years to come to you,* [24]*I hope to see you in passing as I go to Spain, and to be sped on my journey there by you, once I have enjoyed your company for a little.* [25]*At present, however, I am going to Jerusalem with aid for the saints.* [26]*For Macedonia and Achaia have been pleased to make some contribution for the poor among the saints in Jerusalem;* [27]*they were pleased to do it, and indeed they are in debt to them, for if the Gentiles have come to share in their spiritual blessings, they ought also to be of service to them in material blessings.* [28]*When therefore I have completed this, and have delivered to them what has been raised, I shall go on by way of you to Spain;* [29]*and I know that when I come to you I shall come in the fullness of the blessing of Christ.* [30]*I appeal to you, brethren, by our Lord Jesus Christ and by the love of the Spirit, to strive together with me in your prayers to God on my behalf,* [31]*that I may be delivered from the unbelievers in Judea, and that my service for Jerusalem may be acceptable to the saints,* [32]*so that by God's will I may come to you with joy and be refreshed in your company.*

Until now Paul has been preaching the gospel in the eastern Mediterranean region. He now wants to go further west, and has decided on Spain as the goal of his next missionary journey. He wishes to visit the Christian community in Rome on the way to receive help from them for the rest of his journey.

This passage tells us a great deal about Paul's missionary aims. How can he say that he has " no more room for work in these regions "—he is writing from Corinth? We know of about ten years' missionary activity by Paul in the area stretching from Syria to Greece. In the course of this activity Paul concentrated his efforts chiefly on the big towns such as Ephesus, Philippi, Thessalonica and Corinth, but on his journeys he never lost sight of his mission to preach the gospel everywhere. The immediate (and necessary) consequence of his preaching activity was the setting up of Christian communities. The purpose of these communities was to give Christians the necessary help to live a life of faith, and for Paul this always meant help to live in hope of the return of the Lord. His letters were intended to maintain and strengthen this hope. Paul took little interest on the whole in the details of the organization of these communities. Not altogether surprisingly, he expected that the necessary steps would be taken provided that the communities held fast to the essentials of the Christian faith and Christian hope. And no doubt he also presumed that the communities themselves would carry on the missionary work in their pagan surroundings, without the need to draw up their own missionary programmes. The communities and the Christians in them would of themselves arouse interest and win followers through their existence and way of life.

Conclusion of the Letter
(15:33)

Blessing (15:33)

[33]*The God of peace be with you all. Amen.*

Paul ends the announcement of his visit with a short blessing. " The God of peace " (cf. 16:20; 2 Cor. 13:11) is the God who brings about fellowship and unity. Where, humanly speaking, there is small hope for such fellowship and for the success of God's work, God enables men to hope and work against hope. Paul conceived this idea and developed it in his own situation, which was not without its difficulties.

Appendix
(16:1–27)

After the blessing which ends chapter 15, 16:1 marks a fresh start: "I commend to you our sister Phoebe, who is in the service of the community at Cenchreae." There then follows a list of greetings with twenty-six individual names. The list extends from verse 1 to verse 15, and ends with the universal perspective of verse 16, "All the churches of Christ greet you." This in turn seems to be a conclusion, but verse 17 begins again quite abruptly with a warning against divisions and disputes arising from false teachers, although there does not really seem to be sufficient justification in the rest of the letter for such a warning. This short section ends at verse 20 with a blessing, "The grace of our Lord Jesus Christ be with you." It is no longer a surprise to find yet another fresh start: "Timothy, my fellow worker, greets you . . ." and a further seven names are listed. In some manuscripts the list of greetings ends with verse 24, "The grace of our Lord Jesus Christ be with you all. Amen," which is probably a borrowing from 2 Thess. 3:18. The patchwork composition of this chapter is best explained by the suggestion that it consists of fragments of other letters of Paul's which are otherwise unknown to us, put together without any apparent system and later added by an editor of Paul's letters as an appendix to the Epistle to the Romans.